CULTURE SHOCK!

Laos

Stephen Mansfield

Graphic Arts Center Publishing Company
Portland, Oregon

In the same series

Australia	India	Philippines	London at Your Door
Bolivia	Indonesia	Singapore	Rome at Your Door
Borneo	Ireland	South Africa	
Britain	Israel	Spain	A Globe-Trotter's Guide
Burma	Italy	Sri Lanka	A Student's Guide
California	Japan	Sweden	A Traveller's Medical Guide
Canada	Korea	Switzerland	A Wife's Guide
China	Malaysia	Syria	Living and Working Abroad
Czech Republic	Mauritius	Taiwan	Working Holidays Abroad
Denmark	Mexico	Thailand	
Egypt	Morocco	Turkey	
France	Nepal	UAE	
Germany	Netherlands	USA	
Greece	Norway	USA–The South	
Hong Kong	Pakistan	Vietnam	

Illustrations by TRIGG
Photographs by Stephen Mansfield

© 1997 Times Editions Pte Ltd
Reprinted 1998

This book is published by special
arrangement with Times Editions Pte Ltd
Times Centre, 1 New Industrial Road, Singapore 536196
International Standard Book Number 1-55868-301-1
Library of Congress Catalog Number 96-77211
Graphic Arts Center Publishing Company
P.O. Box 10306 • Portland, Oregon 97296-0306 • (503) 226-2402

Printed in Singapore

Negotiate a river by following its bends;
Enter a country by following its customs.
—Indochinese Proverb

A photogenic little model at the Pi Mai festival.

CONTENTS

ACKNOWLEDGEMENTS

It is impossible to thank everyone who gave freely of their knowledge, experience and personal opinions or those who shared their confidential views with me. Ranking among this legion of unofficial contributors are friends, newly made contacts, old Lao hands, people in the business and professional community and countless other helpful sources from all walks of life – dozens of people, both expatriate and Lao, too numerous to mention by name, who gave up their time to field a list of endless and exacting questions. The result of these encounters, and questionnaires of a more specific kind sent out and almost unfailingly returned competed to me, form the basis of *Culture Shock Laos*.

Special thanks must go to veteran residents Monique Mottahedeh and her family whose wisdom, humour and excellent coffee provided much food for thought. An appreciative mention also to Catherine and Mark Paoletti who kindly shared their experiences of other foreign postings in the diplomatic corps, and helped me to review the subject within a wider cultural context. Special mention is also due to Thongphang Manivanh, whose well informed company on many land and aerial explorations over the years is much appreciated.

As it is virtually impossible to put together the definitive version of a book of this sort, comments and contributions from readers are very welcome. The newcomer to Laos, after all, should always have the last say.

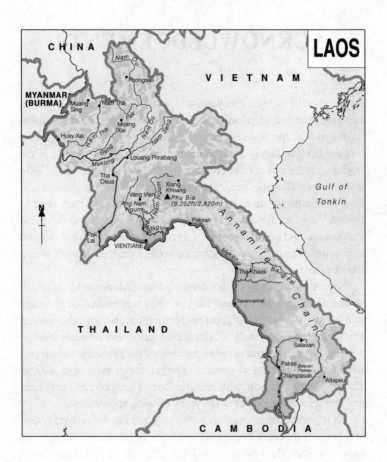

INTRODUCTION

Up to now Lao culture has had very little sustained contact with the outside world. Little wonder that the country has been likened to a hermit crab, one that instinctively withdraws into its fragile carapace at the first sign of encroachment.

There can be few countries left in the world whose names and locations are not immediately recognised. 'Marginal' was how it was first described to me by a businessman passing through the region a few years ago, an epithet that left me eager to know more about this forgotten land. This was easier said than done. Very little appeared to have been written about Laos. History from the Lao point of telling was also in scant supply. Many sources, written on palm leaf manuscripts, have perished through the combined assault of war, climate, insects and the passage of time. Titles that could be found on publisher's lists were mostly political thesis, reports by aid and relief groups like UNICEF, or American military histories. French readers faired rather better as there was a large body of scattered work – histories, ethnographies and studies by colonial administrators and the like – available in French libraries, archives or institutions like the Ecole Francaise d' Extreme-Orient, or the Association Franco-Lao d' Amitie et Solidarite. A few travel accounts were available but the sections on Laos were mostly appendages to more engrossing journeys through Vietnam and Cambodia, the two other countries which, together with Laos, make up the geographical region known as Indo-China. None of this was very helpful for someone arriving in a little known country for the first time.

Natural beauty, a relatively well preserved though increasingly embattled culture and vast areas that have never been seen by a tourist, can only stimulate further interest and inquiry into the country. As technology, education, improved transport networks and just plain curiosity about other races turn the world into even more of a global village than it already is, it becomes increasingly important that we make an effort to understand people from different cultures. There are few better ways to do that than living with people of another country. You wouldn't have bought this book unless you were serious about getting to grips with your new host country.

Contact with outsiders can change cultures as much as the commercial and materialistic values beamed in through the mass media. This book strives to prepare residents for some of the pitfalls involved in living abroad, to give aid and comfort to the bewildered foreigner and to inform you about various customs and services that most people are not immediately aware of. *Culture Shock! Laos* also tries to address itself to one of the most difficult aspects of relocation – learning a new code of nonverbal behaviour and unspoken assumptions that underlie personal and business relationships.

When living in a different culture it is vital to face the disparities in customs and traditions with a positive mind. Humility is an asset. The tendency to place our own culture, ethnicity or personal standards centre stage will set you on a collision course with the host country. Learning to live alongside another culture is one of the most difficult things that can be expected of a human being. You will have to expect communication to be restricted, at least in the early weeks, and social attitudes will be different. Manners and customs may at times seem distant and obtuse, if not downright bizarre. For reasons such as this, it will be best to suspend any and all preconceived notions about what is normal. No amount of forethought can adequately prepare someone for suddenly being in a foreign country without his or her normal support group. It is inevitable therefore, that expatriates experience adjustment problems of one sort or another. These can be minimised, if not headed off altogether, with a combination of realism and preparedness. There is no avoiding culture shock at some level of course, but the impact can be cushioned. Differences in perceptions of the world, family values, the work ethic, marriage, religion and economy – the list is endless – are unavoidable. Encountering these differences though, can be enormously enriching and stimulating, the reward for living in a different culture. Like any good guest you should make an effort to get to know your host. If you try to transplant your own culture in a foreign clime or surround yourself exclusively with the trappings of the expatriate world your opinions and observations will remain shallow and stereotypical.

Relegated until recently to the forgotten or, at best, dimly recalled periphery of Indo-China, Laos is on the brink of change. This book tries to prepare the reader for a culture in rapid, unpredictable transition. It will be a long time before Laos gains an equal footing with other, better known Southeast Asian economic tigers, but change is most definitely afoot. Vientiane, where most foreigners live or are based, is where change is most evident in Laos's evolution from hermit crab to tiger cub. Living in the midst of all these developments, while exciting, can add to the confusion of the new arrival, but you will not be alone. Many Lao are baffled by the changes themselves, suffering, as it were, there own form of culture shock.

Chapter One

THE LAND BETWEEN

It had been predicted that we should have to pass some months in Laos – a region of evil name, protected by the rocks with which its river bristles, and still more by the miasma exhaled by the sun's heat, from the curiosity or ambition of its neighbours.

> —*Travels in Indo-China and the Chinese Empire*, Louis De Carne, 1867

"You're going to live in Lagos!?" a concerned friend asks, barely concealing his surprise and alarm at the prospect. "No. *Laos* ," you answer, "In Asia," hoping to trigger the right response, but this time drawing a complete blank. By this time you are getting used to this sort of conversation, having gone through the same scenario with friends, relatives, the people you are proposing to rent your house to while you are away and the staff at the local branch library where you inquired, unsuccessfully, about titles on Laos.

More worldly acquaintances will admit to having heard of the country but will add to your by now growing sense of unease and premonition with talk of secret wars, Borgia-like political machinations and rumours of goings on behind one of the more inscrutable bamboo curtains of the East. Few countries have been more misunderstood or had their geopolitical history muddled up with that of their neighbours than Laos. Even President Kennedy is known to have announced on national television that Americans might soon be dispatched to a far corner of the world that went by the name of *'Louse,'* or, in the more typically American rendering of the last 30 years, *'Lay-os.'*

Geography will be more in your thoughts at this point however, than phonology. Now that you are about to set foot in the Orient, let's begin by getting properly oriented.

GEOGRAPHY

Laos is a ham-shaped, mountain-segmented country occupying a total area of 91,430 sq. miles, roughly the same size as Britain or the state of Wyoming. Entirely landlocked, Laos is approximately 600 miles long. Its widest point is in the northwest. The southern panhandle of the country narrows to a width of as little as 160 kilometres at some points. Laos sits squarely between Thailand and Myanmar in the west and Vietnam to the east, sharing its northern border with the Chinese province of Yunnan and its southern one with Cambodia. Approximately 70% of the country consists of mountains, highlands and plateaus. The eastern frontier touches one of Indo-China's main geographical features, the Annam Chain, a range of rugged mountains that run from Tibet to Vietnam, slicing up the watersheds of the main east flowing rivers that discharge their waters into the South China Sea. The Dangret ranges and the cataracts at Khone in the south further hinder communication via Cambodia. Only in the west where the Mekong forms a buffer with Thailand's Korat Plateau, is access beyond its own borders relatively easy.

The mountainous northern terrain is noted for its dense jungles, narrow valleys and steep gorges, making it one of the most impassable and least explored areas in the whole of Southeast Asia. Tran Ninh Plateau in the east is a relatively infertile limestone plain of rolling hills and grassland best known for the Plain of Jars, a large scrubland on which hundreds of stone vessels whose origin is still debated, stand. Pou Bia, the country's highest peak at 2,800 metres (9,250 feet), lies just south of here on the edge of the plateau. The east is also home to a spectacular belt of limestone karst rocks, underground rivers and grottoes.

One of the country's most fertile areas, the Bolovens Plateau, lies in the south. Fertile soil, an abundance of rain and a temperate climate allowed the French to grow coffee and rubber trees here. The latex plantations have long gone or fallen into ruin, but the aromatic route from the town of Pakse to Paksone, also celebrated for its durians, is known locally as the Coffee Road. The plateau also supports rice and tobacco as well as many kinds of fruits and vegetables.

Last Eden

Laos is a land of tropical forests. A staggering 50% or more of the country is still covered with primary, rain and monsoon-forest. In this patchwork of dense green, flowers, evergreens, vines, pine, birch, liana, tapang, hornbeam betel, and dozens of other varieties of tree thrive. Birds, reptiles and insects abound in the more inaccessible parts of the forest, particularly in the northeast of Laos. Here hornbills, butterflies, long-horned beetles, bulbuls and pythons find a natural habitat in the distinct micro-climates of each forest. Gibbons, lemurs, wild pigs, loris, rare deer, wild buffalo and many other endangered species like panthers can still be found in the remotest jungles of the Annam Chain.

The harder rainforest trees such as rosewood, teak and sandal-wood are far more vulnerable commercially than those found in the

Spectacular limestone and karst rock formations at Vang Vieng.

monsoon-forests. Although commercial logging has not yet reached the levels found in Thailand or Myanmar the rate of deforestation is increasing as demand grows. Despite the devastation of war and further erosion of the environment by hunters, illegal loggers, over zealous business interests and unscrupulous elements operating within its porous borders, ecologically speaking Laos still merits the epithet of Indo-China's last Eden.

Life Giving Waters

Apart from its mountains and plateaus, the other most dominant geographical feature of Laos is the Mekong River and its eastern tributaries. Most rivers in Laos run a north-south or east-west course. Water is one of the country's main resources and its considerable hydroelectric potential is only just being exploited. In a country with limited road and air services and no railway system whatsoever, the Mekong is of paramount importance. With the exception of the northeastern province of Samneua, the Mekong and its tributaries drain the entire country. Rich topsoil is deposited each year over its banks and the narrow flood plains form the country's wet, rice growing lands. Its fish provide the main protein supplement to the national staple, rice. The 1,600 km of navigable water that passes through Lao territory represents the country's longest single means of communication. Rapids in the far north and south of Laos effectively cut the country off from the sea and limit its cross-border commercial potential.

The Mekong is the longest river in Southeast Asia. On reaching Laos it runs in torrents through a narrow, 200 kilometre long gorge along the Laos-Myanmar frontier, before turning southeast to form a triple border with Thailand, an area better known as the Golden Triangle, one of the world's largest opium producing regions. As the waters become more easily traversed a lively assortment of vessels such as pirogues, sampans, light barges and Chinese tankers appear. The Mekong flows south from here to Sayaboury, the only Lao province to be situated west of the river. After passing the Lao capital of Vientiane, the river curves southeast past Paksane and Thakhek before reaching the major southern towns of Savannakhet and Pakse. The old French settlement of Champassak is the only town of any note before the river cascades over the rocks at Khone and then divides itself into several branches separated by forested islands before exiting into Cambodia. All the country's major city's and settlements are located on or near its banks.

Luang Prabang

The first city of note is Luang Prabang, the former royal capital. Situated on a narrow spit of land at the confluence of the Mekong and Nam Kham rivers, at an elevation of 300 metres above sea level, this provincial city of some 20,000 people remains a veritable, though vulnerable, time capsule. From the wall embrasures of That Chomsi, a golden pagoda perched on the summit of Mount Phousi at the most central point of the city, Luang Prabang looks more like an overgrown kitchen garden replete with temples, monasteries and sanctuaries, than its designation as the cradle of Lao culture.

Luang Prabang first enjoyed temporal power under the rule of Fa Ngum, who in 1353, declared himself King of Lane Xang. The era evokes images less of martial dominance though, than of Laos's distinctive version of Theravada Buddhism, a creed that continues to exert a pervasive and calming influence on Laotian life. Quietly devoted to its past, Luang Prabang has salvaged more from the mayhem of politics and war than any other Lao city, and has largely managed to avoid the seedier aspects of Westernisation – the 'Coca-Colanisation' gladly suffered, some would say actively encouraged, by neighbouring Thailand.

The city prides itself not only on a rich profusion of *wats* (temples), monastic retreats, pleasant half-timbered French houses and an impressive royal palace and museum, but also on its living traditions like *Khao Pakah Din*, a Buddhist ancestor festival, which continues to be celebrated every year. Luang Prabang's most brilliant event is the *Pi Mai*, or New Year festival which falls in mid-April. Many of the original elements of the event, long since discarded in other regions, remain unchanged here. The hushed compounds of temples along Thanon Phothisareth, the main thoroughfare, burst into life over the heady few days of Pi Mai and the garden city pulses with an energy one rarely associates with the pleasantly lackadaisical Lao.

A short pilgrimage to Tham Ting, a 400-year-old cave temple housing hundreds of Buddha statues, some 25 kilometres upstream from Luang Prabang, is a pleasant half day excursion. The river's drainage basin widens here and several tributaries, notably Nam Ou, converge at the spectacular sight of Tham Ting where karst cliffs erupt in a series of gorges. Excursions to secluded monasteries, market towns, weaving villages, the waterfalls at Khouang Sa and the tomb of Henri Mouhot, the French botanist and explorer who died in Luang Prabang from a malaria attack in 1861 are, along with over 30 splendidly preserved temples, some of the sights of Luang Prabang.

Of all Laotian cities, this is the one most vulnerable to inappropriate development. With the resurfacing and upgrading of Route 13 – a tortuous mountain pass subject to landslides and the occasional assault by anti-government rebels and bandits – the prospect looms larger. Until now, the city's physical isolation, the greater levels of poverty in the north, the more orthodox values of this Buddhist diocese and the fact that so little has been written about it have contrived to keep Luang Prabang virtually unchanged for decades. With the upgrading of the town's tiny airport to provide air links with cities in northern Thailand, Vietnam and Yunnan nearing completion, travel operators abroad are slowly catching on to the economic potential of what many consider to be Indo-China's most insouciant and least spoilt city. Hopefully, the prudent residents of Luang Prabang, with assistance and funds from the United Nations who have designated the city a World Heritage site, will insist on a level of development appropriate to their heritage, but with so much

compressed into one small area easily negotiated on foot, the flawless beauty and cultural assets of Luang Prabang represent a strong temptation to tour group promoters and related business interests in the region. Luang Prabang is a sleeping beauty about to be roused from its slumber.

Vientiane

The 400,000 strong capital of Vientiane, or Vieng Chan as it is to the Lao, is divided into a series of *ban* , or small villages usually built around the local temple or wat, and larger districts called *muang* , meaning townships. The four main districts are Muang Chanthebouli in the north, Muang Sisatatanak in the south and Muang Xaisettha and Sikhottabong to the east and west.

As the increasingly important political and commercial hub of the nation, most of the ministries, embassies, consulates, overseas development agencies, non government organisations and large bodies like the United Nations, UNESCO and Unicef, have their headquarters here. It also houses the largest number of commercial banks, airline offices, tour companies and travel agencies as well as shops, hotels, restaurants, business and commercial centres, hospitals, packers and shippers, the country's only university, Dong-Dok, and a small international airport at Wat Tay.

King Settathirat transferred the capital here from Luang Prabang in 1563 to protect the kingdom of Lane Xang from invasions by the Siamese, Burmese and later, the Vietnamese. The strategically improved site of the new capital on the banks of the Mekong, closer to the centres of trade and more defensible, was endowed with a number of palaces, libraries and Buddhist monuments, including the impressive wats of That Luang and Wat Phra Keo, a museum-like temple erected to house the Emerald Buddha, the palladium of the kingdom, which was brought from Chiang Mai. The illustrious Soukham statues were brought down from Luang Prabang for safekeeping and to enhance the prestige of the new capital. By the beginning of the 19th century Vientiane had become a flourishing city. Anger and grievances over foreign control and intervention however, came to a violent head in 1826 with an open rebellion led by the Lao king Chao Anou. With the recapture of Vientiane by the Siamese, the city suffered a terrible sacking and many buildings were put to the torch. If the accounts of contemporary travellers are accurate, Vientiane never recovered the cultural and artistic brilliance it once enjoyed in its heyday as a royal city and centre of Buddhism.

To the French who colonised the country Laos came the closest to their ideal of an earthly paradise in Southeast Asia. But if Laos ever really resembled a kind of landlocked Tahiti, the Vietnam War put an abrupt end to it. For more than 10 years Laos was a battleground for America's secret war in Indo-China. As the conflict in Laos escalated, Vientiane soon became the centre for covert American operations in the region. In recent years Vientiane was again relegated to little more than a mildly interesting detour on the way to or from more ascendant cities in the region like Bangkok, Phnom Penh or Hanoi. Many visitors however, happy to escape the frantic traffic, air pollution, crime and sex trade that characterise many other Southeast Asian capitals, are charmed by Vientiane, a city where not long ago, pedicabs and bicycles outnumbered cars and trucks.

Vientiane, one of the few Asian capitals not to be choked with car fumes.

Even now Vientiane continues to cast a spell over the visitor. Dilapidated colonial villas with blue-louvred windows and airy balconies stand in the middle of small banana groves, many under the restoration orders of Vientiane's *nouveau riche comprador* class of traders, shopkeepers, middlemen and brokers for the increasing number of foreign businessmen seeking investment opportunities in Laos. After years of seclusion and stagnation the pace of change and economic development evident in Vientiane is doubtless on the increase but not at a rate, government officials are keen to stress, that will harm the Laotian way of life. An Australian funded bridge connecting Nong Khai in Thailand with a spot downstream from Vientiane, completed in 1994, is certain to be an enormous harbinger of change, one that is already putting Indo-China's smallest and most obscure capital back on the map. Vientiane's days of invisibility are coming to an end.

The Road South

A well surfaced road, Route 13, takes visitors south from Vientiane through the modest commercial town of Paksane to another Mekong town, Thakhek, also known by its old name, Khammouane. Excursions to fabulous limestone caves, grottoes and rock formations nearby, to Wat Sikhotaboun, a temple built by Chao Anou, the magnificent setting of the town itself and the return of commercial traffic with the completion and upgrading of Route 13, auger well for this former colonial trading post.

The largest town in southern Laos, with a population of well over 50,000, is Savannakhet, the provincial capital of the province of the same name. Referred to by the Lao simply as Savan, the city is the second largest in Laos. It is also an important river port for trade with Thailand and a major transportation hub linking Thailand, via Route 9, with the Vietnamese port of Danang. Savan has the largest Chinese community in the country, a presence adding to its brisk, entrepreneurial character.

I once heard an Australian engineer occupying the seat behind me on one of my flights to Pakse making a valiant effort to overcome an obvious fear of flying (sooner or later everyone ends up using planes to get around) by resorting to humour. "The good news," he was telling the passenger beside him, "is that, in the event of an emergency landing, the plain below is almost entirely flat. The bad news? It's covered in secondary forest!" And so it is. Rich alluvial plains and yet-to-be despoiled forests characterise this magnificent region of Laos.

Towards the bottom of the southern panhandle, located at the confluence of the Mekong and Xe Dong rivers, the 25,000 strong former colonial town of Pakse is a busy commercial and administrative centre for the region. Pakse is known locally for its excellent market and its local crafts, particularly its exquisite woven silk textiles. The town's importance stems from its designation as a major keystone to the southern route, its position at the crossroads to both Vietnam and Cambodia. The French, resigning themselves to the fact that Laos would never be more than the back garden of their empire in Indo-China, built just the bare essentials needed to run this part of the country. These included a post office, church, a small quay, a bridge built to military specifications, and several handsome villas, described to me by one Leningrad educated Lao as 'dachas.' Few visitors come to this region except for professional reasons, but those who do make it to the south come to visit the lush Bolovens Plateau or to see the important archeological site of Wat Phu, a 7th century Khmer ruin close to the village of Champassak. Wat Phu's spectacular location, surrounded by a thick canopy of katou and rain trees, can have changed little since the French explorer Francis Garnier discovered it in 1866. Foreign residents, ideally placed to do so, are strongly recommended while they are in the country to set aside time to visit this marvellous monument.

Part of the splendid ruins at Wat Phu in southern Laos.

POPULATION

With a population estimated at slightly under five million, Laos is one of the most sparsely populated areas of Southeast Asia, a fact that has impeded its economic development as well as its ability to defend itself against the ambitions of demographically superior neighbours. The nations population density is around 47 people per square mile. Population density is highest in those provinces which contain the largest land masses of alluvial soil – Vientiane, Savannakhet and Saravane. The government is trying to redress the situation by encouraging population growth which at present is at 3.1% annually. Despite a higher than average child mortality rate, children represent a large proportion of the population now. According to the World Health Organisation, average life expectancy in 1995 stood at 50.3 years.

Roughly 80% of the population are involved in some form of subsistence farming. Though there has been no major trend towards urbanisation in Laos this is likely to change significantly with the growth of private sector enterprise in large towns, cities and some border areas experiencing a brisk cross-border trade, and improvements in road transport. Urban statistics are subject to fluctuations but Vientiane and its municipal environs are said to have 378,000 inhabitants; Luang Prabang 20,000; Savannakhet 52,000; and Pakse 21,000.

Broadly speaking there are four main ethnic groups in Laos (see Chapter Six): Lao Lum, the dominant lowlanders, who account for slightly over half the population; Lao Thai; Lao Theung, the country's midlanders, and Lao Soung, its highlanders. The latter group includes most of the nation's most bodacious hill tribes and many of its minority groups. The province with the greatest ethnic diversity is Luang Nam Tha in the far northwest., which is said to be home to 39 distinct tribes.

After the Communist takeover of 1975, over 300,000 Lao – about 8% of the total population – fled the country. Some were resettled abroad, though many found themselves in the limbo of refugee camps on the Thai-Lao and Cambodia borders. Today, the number of returnees exceeds the number of emigres.

CLIMATE

Temperatures are tropical to subtropical, varying with altitude, latitude and the monsoon. Three distinct seasons characterise the monsoonal climate of Laos but there is considerable variation between districts according to latitude and elevation. During the dry season which runs from November to April, less than 5 centimetres of rain a month fall on the Vientiane plain which receives an average rainfall of as high as 30 centimetres a month from May to October. Average rainfalls vary quite a bit across the country with Luang Prabang getting about 125 centimetres and the Bolovens Plateau as much as 250 centimetres a year. Temperatures can drop to below freezing point, especially in December and January in places like Xieng Khouane province. Even in the lowland cities of the flood plains evenings and nights can be quite cool.

The humid period sees temperatures rise to above 40°C in March and April. If you are lucky these peak heat months are relieved by the 'mango showers' – short, unannounced deluges of rain. April and May are certainly the stickiest months, caused largely by an increase in storm clouds. The rainy season begins in May and, until October, the average temperature is around 29°C. June, July and August are the wettest months, the monsoonal rains resulting in the much anticipated inundation of the Mekong and its tributaries which is essential to the life sustaining wet-rice cultivation of Laos. When the Lao are, along with most of the agricultural communities from East Africa to China, waiting and praying for the life giving rains to reach their corner of the Indo-Chinese peninsula, most expatriates, unless they have a predilection for humidity, eagerly await the advent of the more temperate November weather and the chance to slip on a light sweater or jacket and dream of cooler climes.

THE ECONOMY

Under the French, little practical importance was placed on the creation of a viable Lao economy. French efforts were devoted primarily to the construction of a road network designed to facilitate the political and military administration of the region. Laos effectively remained little more than a reserve pool of incompletely explored and almost entirely unexploited natural and human resources.

Today, Laos remains one of the poorest and most under developed countries in the world. Poverty is endemic and standards of health and education are among the lowest in Southeast Asia. Major impediments to economic growth include an inadequate infrastructure of roads and telecommunications, a poorly trained workforce, an absence of skilled managers, capital and foreign exchange, low population density, a rugged terrain and a per capita annual income of only US$240.

Most towns lack modern sewage and only major cities or villages located near hydroelectric plants receive more than a few hours of electricity per day. Being entirely landlocked has restricted its export potential until now as the cost involved in transshipment through Thailand or Vietnam dramatically increases the price of Lao goods, making them less competitive on the international market. Laos remains one of the only nations in the world without a railway system.

Overseas Development Aid

The aid vacuum left by the withdrawal of the Soviets is being rapidly filled by such donors as the IMF, the World Bank, the Asian Development Bank and a number of NGOs. Japanese, Swedish and Australian governments are the biggest development aid donors in Laos. Over a quarter of Laos's GDP – double the nation's export earnings – now come from foreign aid, much of which finances the import of essential foreign goods such as food, oil and machinery, which Laos, without a significant manufacturing base of its own, is heavily dependent upon. Described as one of the highest per capita aid flows in the developing world, Vientiane's ability to absorb an inflow of funds on this scale is being sorely tested.

Natural Resources

As much as 80% of the labour force is still engaged in agriculture. Rice is the main food staple with cassava and maize cultivated as substitutes. The principal agricultural areas are found on the Mekong flood plains near Vientiane and Savanakhet where the volume of rice and soy bean production has increased by over 30% in recent years. Coffee, cotton, sugar cane, cardamom and tobacco are significant agricultural products grown on the Bolovens Plateau and on slopes where detrimental slash-and-burn farming by shifting cultivators has been successfully reduced in recent years. Livestock and fisheries are also showing some sign of promise.

Laos has an abundance of largely untapped natural resources including forests, minerals and a hydroelectric potential second to none in Southeast Asia. Tourism is another source of income almost as potentially lucrative as energy. An important source of foreign exchange for Laos are the receipts collected from over flight rights, with over 80 international flights passing through Lao airspace per day. Along with timber processing and electricity, the garments industry has become one of Laos's leading export earners.

Factories as such employ a very small percentage of the workforce engaged, for the main part, in low-key enterprises like tobacco processing, soft drinks manufacturing, brewing and the making of rubber shoes and slippers. Cotton and silk weaving, and pottery production remain very much at the cottage industry level.

NEW REALITIES, NEW ALLIANCES

The redrawing of the world's geopolitical map, the ensuing economic chaos in the Soviet Union and the withdrawal of financial backers in Hanoi have forced Laos to introduce economic reforms, explore new markets in the capitalist world and improve its historically troubled relations with neighbouring Thailand. The collapse of Soviet aid, which at one time accounted for as much as 80% of Laos's budget, and the need to establish an economy that matches up to minimum international standards, has also involved more fundamental nation-building reforms. These include the founding of a proper legal infrastructure that includes commercial property and tax laws, as well as such institutions as a central bank, all essential requisites for any modern society.

Much credit is due to the government for loosening the straight jacket of Marxist-Stalinist economics as early as 1986, when the state sensibly backed down from its unpopular policy of agricultural collectivism. With its more recent and far reaching program of reforms, known as *chin tanakan mai* , or 'new thinking,' the government has allowed farmers to own their land and sell crops at free market prices, a measure that has stimulated farmers to plant more and helped to establish a reasonable level of food self sufficiency. The government has also freed trade, floated the kip, the national currency, eased interest rates, leased or sold off many top heavy or unprofitable state owned enterprises and opened up foreign invest-ment by liberalising banking systems and the foreign investment code. To the government's further credit, Vientiane represents an economic rebirth in which everyone who is able and willing may participate, including those who fled the country in 1975 or those interned in remote re-education camps.

Strategies For The Future

While these reforms have won the praise of international institutions like the IMF and Asian Development Bank, and encouraged countries like Thailand and Singapore to support Laos's membership of ASEAN, many problems still remain. One of these is settling on what kind of economy Laos should have, since it clearly lacks the capacity to follow the export driven policies of countries like China, Thailand or

Taiwan. The country and its foreign advisers and strategists are concentrating on four principal and distinct areas for generating wealth in the near future. The first is mining and energy. Laos generates something like 250 megawatts of hydroelectric power, 75% of which is exported to Thailand. The government plans to add between 1500 and 2000 MW by the end of the century. One of the largest in a number of proposed dams is the 700 MW Nam Theun 2 dam, southeast of Vientiane, slated to cost US$1.2 billion. With Laos in the best of all possible positions to tap the hydroelectric resources of the Mekong, with a potential to generate as much as 20,000 MW of power, the country is already being dubbed the 'battery' of Southeast Asia.

The largely untapped mineral resources in Laos include proven reserves of gold, gemstones, bauxite, lignite, gypsum, limestone, potash, coal, and a deposit of iron ore so dense in one mountain region that American bombers heading for Vietnam during the war found their navigational instruments prone to erratic responses. A number of Western countries are now engaged in prospecting for minerals, oil and gas.

The second strategy being looked at concerns agriculture and forestry. The raising of cattle and feed grains is already well under way. Laos has something like two million hectares of virgin forest, much of which is valuable, much sought after hardwood like teak. The government proposes to end the export of raw timber and replace it with a processed wood industry which could make Laos a major exporter of pulp and paper. In spite of this, heavy deforestation continues. Much of this is illegal logging which distant, money-strapped Vientiane is powerless to do much about. The government has tried to combat the piracy of its forests by delegating more responsibility for the upkeep, as well as land tenures, to local villages in the hope that they will appropriate sustainable amounts of timber for their own uses. In this way they become more dependent upon the woods as a long term resource whose conservation they will come to perceive as being linked to their own interests and well being. Reservations about the country's future at the hands of outsiders were succinctly expressed by Prince Panya Souvanna Phouma, son of the former prime minister, an unlikely admirer of the government's cautious approach to environmental development. "Do you want them to be workers in hotels?" he asked, alluding to the poorer strata of Lao society: "Do you want them to cut down their forests? Is it economic progress when the hilltribes in Thailand become beggars in Thailand?" A vision of Lao minorities fetching and carrying for Vientiane's nouveau riche is not as far fetched as it sounds. The penury of the more transient minorities is easily traded for demeaning but tempting jobs in the burgeoning urban service industry.

Part of this private service sector involves tourism, the third economic strategy currently being examined and feasibility tested. Until now, Laos has discouraged large scale tourism, preferring limited, high-end tourism with its low impact on indigenous culture and values. The government continues, with some justification, to remain wary about encouraging too many visitors and visas to enter the country are costly and not available on arrival as they are in many other countries in the region. Laos however, could find a suitable middle way by following the path of eco-tourism which a number of other developing countries have benefited from. Countries increasingly sought out as destinations for this kind of tourism are those which can offer an exemplary natural environment, an intriguing

history and an authentic living culture, a unique combination found only in a few remaining parts of Southeast Asia, Laos being one of them. Preserving the appeal of Lao culture is easier said than done. Although there is clearly money to be made out of the past, once people begin to reap its benefits they increasingly want to live in the future. This is the almost insoluble dilemma facing the Lao government and their UN advisers in their pursuit of cultural tourism.

The last of the economic strategies for the future would be to see the country playing the role of a service centre or way-station for transport, power and telecommunications links between China, Thailand, Vietnam and Cambodia, a plan that even its most enthusiastic advocates admit would take decades to complete. In the creation of what has optimistically been termed the 'Golden Quadrangle,' an economic cooperative would bring Thailand, Laos, Myanmar and southern China together. Landlocked and underdeveloped Laos is seen as a keystone to the success of a scheme approved by the ADB to build overland corridors between Bangkok and Yunnan and another route to the deep sea port of Da Nang in Vietnam. With the skeleton of a north-south route already in existence, the advent of the Thai-Lao Mithraphab (Friendship) Bridge across the Mekong has meant that it is now possible, in theory, to drive all the way from Singapore to Beijing. Many temperamentally prudent Lao however, fear that the bridge and similar collaborations with Thailand in particular, could become conduits for deforestation, water pollution, corruption, prostitution and excessive Westernisation.

BRIDGING THE GAP: LAOS AND THAILAND

An imposing construction based on a balanced and segmented cantilever, the 1174 metre bridge connects the northeastern Thai city of Nong Khai with the Lao port of Tha Nalaeng, 19 kilometres southeast of Vientiane. The bridge, the first of its kind to span the Mekong, boasts two traffic lanes, a walkway and provision for a central railway track should Laos decide to build its own railway network at some time. The pointedly named 'Friendship Bridge' symbolises an attempt to build bridges between two countries whose relations have not always been easy. An historical distrust of Thailand is particularly strong among the people of Vientiane province who suffered a vengeful sacking at the hands of the Thai general Mom Ghao Thap who, in 1827, was charged with Rama III's order "to return Vieng Chan to the wild animals and leave nothing behind but weeds and water." Thai mercenaries were among the ranks of the CIA's secret army; American B-52s took off on their bombing runs over Laos from bases in Thailand, and in the late 1980s a bitter border dispute unleashed fresh animosity between the two neighbours. The Lao resent the common assumption among Thais that their country is merely an extension of Isaan province in northern Thailand and the Lao younger siblings of the Thai. It is hardly surprising to learn that one of the rallying calls of the revolution was *Laos pen Lao* – "Laos for the Lao."

Despite the entrenched mistrust, the current entente cordial makes perfect sense. The two nations, sharing an almost identical language and ethnicity, would appear to have much in common. The new mood on both sides of the Mekong was neatly summed up in one former Thai prime minister's rallying call – "From the battlefield to the marketplace," a leitmotif being enthusiastically taken up all over Indo-China.

Thailand is the largest foreign investor in Laos. The majority of logging contracts have been awarded to Thai companies and traders over the river who also provide most of Laos's processed food and consumer goods. The main bulk of the country's foreign earnings now come from Thailand and the lion's share of farm exports, like electricity, are destined for the Thai market. Several Thai banks have branches in Vientiane, and many contracts such as telecommunications concessions, have been awarded to Thai firms. In tourism as well, Thailand is likely to remain the main gateway into Laos. Laos is seen by many Thai businessmen as a useful location for transplanting some of its own labour intensive industries, especially the agricultural and textile sectors. The country's political stability is an attractive asset in this respect.

For many Lao, especially the young, Western progress has become synonymous with Thailand. Many Lao youths are bedazzled by Thai pop culture and its immensely popular commercial TV programs which can be picked up all along the Lao side of the Mekong. Many people now read readily available Thai books and magazines. Many older Laos, are uncomfortable with the country's changing relationship to its closest neighbour and the economic and cultural attitudes slowly infiltrating Vientiane, but accept that a significant Thai business presence in their country is inevitable if Laos's open door economic policies are to continue.

Old enmities are being eased however, not only by much needed Thai investment and a modest foreign aid program run by the Thai government but also by the Thai King, Bhumibol Ayulyadej, and members of his family who have made genuine, much appreciated efforts to bridge the gap between the two countries.

— *Chapter Two* —

HISTORY LESSONS

For the Lao people, the invisible link with the nation, the nationhood, is inborn and transmitted from generation to generation.

—Mayoury Ngaosyvathn

The geopolitical priorities facing Laos today – the quest for national and ethnic unity, the preservation of its fragile culture and resistance to foreign domination – are hardly any different now than they were at the time of its earliest recorded history. The story of Laos is synonymous with the history of the Lao themselves. Despite successive waves of foreign invaders who have tried to impose their own cultural values on the country, a distinct and unique Lao identity has survived miraculously intact.

Until relatively recently, the majority of Lao learnt about their past from monks and balladeers. Versions of history differ though. Laos consists of a vast number of ethnic tribes many of whom, without the benefit of written scripts, have relied traditionally upon orally transmitted and memorised foundation legends to explain their origins and historical evolution.

EARLY ACCOUNTS

According to one Lao legend, the semi-divine Khoun Borom descended to earth mounted on a white elephant, furnished with all the accoutrements of royalty, where, near the site of Dien Bien Phu in present day Vietnam, he found a vine bearing two large gourds. When pierced, men, women, animals and seed emerged, instantly populating the world. Khoun Boron's seven sons divided the land seven ways and the kingdoms and fiefdoms of the Thai peoples were established. The historically verified migratory routes of the Thai people, of which the Lao are one, correspond with remarkable accuracy to these seven domains.

The Lao entered history at a later date than other Thai races like the Shan, Siamese and Lu, but the pattern of infiltration and settlement appears to have been almost identical. The Lao originally seem to have enjoyed a shared occupancy of a large area of southern China centred around the present day provinces of Yunnan and Sikang. By the 8th century a strong military kingdom, Nan Chao, had been established in western Yunnan. The slow southern migration of the Thai people into the Indo-Chinese peninsula was accelerated in the middle of the 13th century with the invasion of Kublai Khan's army and its capture of the Nan Chao capital in 1253.

LAND OF A MILLION ELEPHANTS

The recorded history of Laos begins with the reign of Fa Ngum (1353–73), who spent much of his youth at the Khmer court of Angkor with his father, an exiled prince from Muong Swa. There he married a Khmer princess and was converted to Theravada Buddhism, an event that was to have an enormous influence on Lao culture. When Fa Ngum's father died he reclaimed Moung Swa and quickly set about making his new faith the official religion, receiving a mission of scholars, monks and craftsmen who brought with them numerous sacred books and a gold Buddha statue, originally from Sri Lanka,

The figure of a 17th century Dutch visitor to Laos has been recorded on the door of a temple in Luang Prabang.

called the Phra Bang. This diminutive statue, a replica of which is displayed once a year during the Lao New Year festival, remains to this day the single most revered religious symbol in Laos and the palladium of the nation.

Fa Ngum's insatiable appetite for war and successes in his eastern and western campaigns resulted in the rapid expansion of Lao territory. This now included all of present day Laos and large areas of northern and eastern Thailand. In 1353 these conquests were consolidated into the first truly united Lao state, the kingdom of Lane Xang, meaning the Land of a Million Elephants and the White Parasol. Fa Ngum's successes, and excesses, were to prove his undoing. A war weary and militarily oppressed nation conspired to have him deposed in 1373.

He was succeeded by Samsenthai, a title meaning Lord of Three Hundred Thousand Thai, a reference to the figure of a national census ordered by the king. Samsenthai was a man of peace, an organiser and consolidator who devoted much effort to building pagodas, enhancing the status of the Buddhist clergy and establishing a long lasting administrative structure. Before Lane Xang's neighbours, embroiled in their own disputes, were aware of what was happening, the new kingdom, expanding along the borders of the declining Khmer Empire, had grown into a powerful independent kingdom of its own.

Despite the odd incursion by the Annamese, a long period of peace followed in which a powerful but underpopulated Lane Xang was able to consolidate its position through trade and intermarriage, particularly with the powerful Siamese court based at Ayutthaya. This period was ruled by King Photisarath, a devout Buddhist who tried unsuccessfully, to put an end to the spirit cults and rituals which form the basis of some of the animistic practices which are still widespread in Laos today, especially in rural areas. By seizing the throne of Chiang Mai, Photisarath set the dominant regional powers of Southeast Asia on a collision course that was to continue for the rest of the century.

After an abortive attempt by the Siamese to dislodge Photisarath's son, Setthathirath, from the throne, the expansionist Burmese, seeing Chiang Mai as an ideal base from which to carry on their operations against Ayutthaya, launched two further attacks on Lane Xang. Setthathirath in the meantime had returned to Lane Xang with the prestigious Emerald Buddha, a green jasper carving and a much coveted symbol of sovereignty. In the ensuing fifty years of Setthathirath's reign, until his mysterious disappearance while on an expedition in Attopeu, the three way struggle between Siam, Burma and Lane Xang did much to weaken the kingdom. With Setththirath gone, the Burmese were easily able to subjugate the country, which they did for the next twenty years until resurgent Siamese forces were able to push them back and at the same time, bring Chiang Mai under their control.

GOLDEN AGE

After a succession of non-dynastic rulers, Souligna Vongsa, Lane Xang's 'Sun King,' was elected to the throne in 1637 and, for a period of 57 years, generally regarded by the Lao as the peak of their Golden Age, the country was able to regain much of its strength and political standing. It was also able to establish secure borders by means of peaceful treaties. The boundary with Annam, for example, was agreed upon on ethnic grounds: land settled on by people living in "houses on piles and verandahs" would belong to Lang Xang, while those occupied by people in homes "without piles or verandahs" would be deemed to belong to Annam.

It was at this time that Lane Xang experienced its first contact with Europeans, the most famous being Gerrit van Wusthoff, a Dutchman who arrived on a diplomatic and trade mission and went on to publish an account of his journey to Laos. Other visitors, such as the Italian priest Filippo de Marini, also provided fascinating records of their encounters with the beauty of Vientiane, the customs of the Lao and the formal splendour of the court.

Decline of Lane Xang

Sadly, Souligna Vongsa's long and illustrious reign ended in calamity. Refusing to stay the execution of his only son, accused of adultery, he effectively propelled the country into a power struggle for the succession which saw Lane Xang divided into three rival kingdoms. The first of these was established in Luang Prabang in 1707. Another prince set up his kingdom at Champassak in the south and a third kingdom came into existence in a large area centred around Vientiane.

Internal quarrels and struggles to maintain their independence against outside forces characterise the history of Laos in the 18th and 19th centuries. Annamese invasions from the east, Burmese from the west, Chinese intrusions and successive waves of bandits from the north culminated in 1778 with the temporary loss of Vientiane and the subsequent vassalage of Laos to the Siamese and Annamese. A failed rebellion led by king Chao Anou against the Siamese led to the sacking and virtual obliteration of Vientiane in 1827. In accord with the age old Southeast Asian practice of warfare, in which occupied territory was systematically depopulated and its inhabitants forcefully resettled, vast numbers of Lao prisoners were sent to Bangkok. Chao Anou was taken to the Thai capital where he was displayed to the public in a cage. Traditionally regarded as a traitor by the Thais but revered until now as a national hero by the Lao, the case of Chao Anou is a good example of how historical perspectives can diverge between two nations.

Luang Prabang also suffered from conflicts with Burma, Siam and Vientiane. Marauding bands called Black and Yellow Flags, fleeing the Tai Ping rebellion in south China, sacked and plundered the city and the eastern province of Tran Ninh (Xieng Khouane). With the establishment of a French protectorate in Annam in 1884, the Siamese, eager to head off any encroachment into Laos, began strengthening its control over the country, reducing the kings of Luang Prabang and Champassak to the status of governors directly answerable to Siamese commissioners installed at their courts.

COLONIAL LAOS

By 1884 the French had annexed Cochin China, established a protectorate in Cambodia and successfully concluded treaties making further protectorates in Tonkin and Annam. Laos was next in line for the same treatment. In a move to forestall French efforts to revive former Annamese claims to large areas of Lao territory, the Siamese invaded Xieng Khouane and Houa Phans under the pretext of protecting ethnically Thai regions from the Chinese dacoits, a ruse that became less convincing when the viceroy of Luang Prabang was removed to Bangkok as a hostage. Ensuing negotiations between the Siamese and the French secured the Europeans the right to maintain a vice-consul in Luang Prabang. Auguste Pavie is generally credited with securing Laos for the French, having persuaded the royal court at Luang Prabang that their best interests would be served by accepting French 'protection.' All claims by the Siamese were withdrawn in 1893 when France concluded a treaty formally bringing Laos into the Union of Indo-China. Territorial claims between the French and British were settled in 1896 with the conclusion of a treaty making the Mekong the border between Laos and Burma, a move effectively designating Laos as a buffer state between Britain and France's respective empires in the East. The Mekong was set as the boundary between Laos and Siam and, in 1905, further treaties ceded west bank portions of Luang Prabang and the province of Bassac to the Siamese. Tens of thousands of Lao suddenly found themselves subject to Siam. Today, large numbers of ethnic Lao continue to live in the northeast provinces of Thailand.

The king was permitted to stay in Luang Prabang but all important administrative decisions were made by the French *resident-superieur* in Vientiane and a vice-consul in Luang Prabang. By and large, French rule in Laos was less severe than in their other Indo-Chinese colonies. The royal family was respected and patterns of local rule, customs and traditions went largely unchanged, except when they were incompatible with larger French objectives. The style of administration has been aptly described as 'benign neglect.' To the chagrin of the Lao however, the French brought in large numbers of Annamese (Vietnamese) as labourers and minor bureaucrats. The move was much resented by the Lao who have always harboured a mistrust for these 'people from the other side of the mountains.' An inherent animosity towards the Vietnamese continues to this day among the ordinary Lao. For the next fifty years or more of colonial rule Laos, quietly consigned to the back garden of France's Indo-Chinese empire, left little imprint on history.

Independence Movements

Laos was shaken from its reverie by the invasion and occupation of Indo-China by the Japanese in 1941. These new Asian invaders chose to administer Laos through the Vichy government but the obvious inability of France to protect Laos from the Japanese was a severe blow to French prestige. The surrender of the Japanese in August 1945 encouraged a seminal Lao independence movement known as the *Lao Issara* (Free Lao) to press for unconditional independence from the French. The leader of the movement, Prince Phetsarath, formed a government in Vientiane and on September 1, 1945, declared Lao independence. France refused to recognise the new state and quickly set about crushing Lao resistance. King Sisavang Vong sided with the French who reoccupied Laos and crowned him as constitutional head of its new protectorate in 1946. The entire Lao Issara government took refuge over the river and, with the support of Ho Chi Minh's guerrilla movement in Vietnam, a government in exile under Prince Phetsarath, was set up in Bangkok. Increasing national-istic pressure over the following years obliged France to grant Laos formal independence within the French Union in July, 1949. Full sovereignty was granted four years later after France's extraordinary defeat by the Viet Minh at Dien Bien Phu in northern Vietnam sounded the death knell of French colonialism in the East.

Foreign Affairs

No sooner had the French left than Laos found itself being drawn inexorably into the affairs not only of its immediate neighbours but the conflicting ideologies of the superpowers. Indo-China became the designated ground on which the USA, China and the USSR tested their military and political theories. The political situation within Laos itself was also rapidly deteriorating as a three-way split, between Prince Souvanna Phouma, a staunch neutralist and official head of the government, Prince Boun Oum of Champassak, a right-wing American sympathiser, and Prince Souvannouvong, better known as the 'Red Prince,' and a key figure in the newly formed Pathet Lao resistance movement, threatened to plunge the country into further chaos. With America embarking upon a CIA backed secret war in Laos aimed at preventing Communist integration in Indo-China, Vientiane quickly became a centre for covert American undercover operations throughout the region.

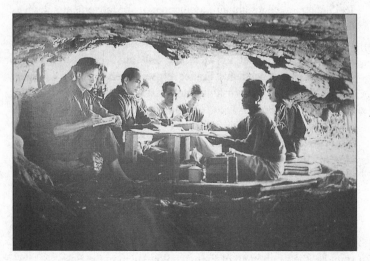

The limestone caves at Sam Nuea were used during the 'secret war' in Laos as Pathet Lao headquarters, communication centres and even hospitals.

The war was largely an aerial operation fought with immoderate quantities of bombs, herbicides and defoliants. Before the bombing was halted in 1973, a total of 2,093,100 tons of explosives had been dropped on Laos, an average of 177 sorties a day or, to put it differently, the equivalent of one plane load of deadly munitions every eight minutes for nine years. The legacy of these policies continues today with between five and ten people either killed or injured each month from unexploded munitions.

In the wake of the Pathet Lao Communist victory of 1975 and the dissolution of the monarchy, a flood of refugees, including many of the country's intelligentsia and technicians, fled over the Mekong into camps in Thailand, from where some were eventually successful in finding asylum in countries like France, the United States and Japan. In a more accommodating post Cold War era where deals and concessions are more important than doctrinaire political ideologies, a growing number of former exiles are returning to their homeland to be reunited with their families, start businesses and recover confiscated property. Becoming Lao citizens once more, they are able to participate in the more liberal economic climate now helping to define and shape the country's relations with the outside world.

43

SAVOURING THE PAST

Now that you know at least the salient facts about Lao history you might like to explore it in more concrete ways. Most Lao cities are small enough to be negotiated comfortably on foot or by bicycle, a far more revealing way to discover and savour the remains of the past than with a high speed vehicle. Laos in any case, is not really made for high speed. Slow motion more like it!

The notion of safety in numbers does not really apply in Lao cities which boast some of the most crime free sidewalks in the world. Traffic is still blissfully tame by comparison with almost anywhere else in Southeast Asia.

Although you are unlikely to find yourself hopelessly lost for very long even in Vientiane, arm yourself with a good map to start. There are few visible street signs, although all the roads, even the smallest, appear to have names. The Mekong river, the country's historical lifeline, and temples, its spiritual centres, are the main landmarks in most Lao towns of any size. Most of the old or important buildings and institutions in Vientiane and Luang Prabang – the morning market, post office, old royal palace and presidential building – are found within minutes of the river.

A fragrance of the past lingers in the great temples, libraries and sanctuaries of Vientiane like Wat Simaung where a Khmer stone is revered as the founding pillar of the city, or at Wat Sisaket, one of the only temples to have been left unscathed during the raising of Vientiane by the Thais at the beginning of the 19th century. Drop into one of the antique shops or galleries selling textiles along any main boulevard and you will find design motifs and scroll figures that can be traced back to an earlier Laos of legends, spirit worship and the supernatural.

Start looking for French influences and you will find them everywhere – in crumbling, stucco-faced villas near the river, faded signs above shop doors, the habit of older *cadres* (a French word used by the Lao to denote government official) of addressing foreigners in

French before switching to English, and in the crisp, perfectly baked baguettes sold from *ambulants* all over the city and much favoured by the Lao for breakfast.

Traces of more recent history are easily sought out if you have an interest in such things. Quarter S, also known as Silver City, and now simply called KM-6, is where CIA agents and Air America pilots once lived. There are several monuments to battles, rebellions and revolutions and a rather rundown looking Soviet Embassy. Old cars – it's fascinating to speculate who might have driven this old Peugeot or that ancient Benz – can sometimes be seen, and heard, puttering along the dusty streets of the town.

History can be misleading though. Someone recently estimated that there were no more than 500 elephants left in Laos, not much for a country once known as the Land of a Million Elephants. Keep your

Children playing on the shells of B-52 bombs dropped on Laos in the late 1960s and early 70s.

ears open for forthcoming festivals and special events like the Lao New Year and the That Luang Festival with their colourful elephant parades and you might get to see one of the symbols of Lane Xang.

People are fond of describing Laos as Southeast Asia's last Shangri-la, another rather misleading epithet. Shangri-las, after all, are usually the optimistic figments of other people's imaginations, certainly not the stuff of everyday reality experienced by the Lao or foreign resident. Nevertheless, Laos often feels like a quaint rural backwater where the distinction between past and present is often apt to be blurred, its towns urban time capsules of immense charm. Living in a time slip however, like experiencing a different form of gravity can sometimes, as any astronaut will tell you, be a mixed blessing.

— Chapter Three —

FEET IN THE STREET

"Now those are *really* old stupas!"

—Overheard comment made by a tourist on first seeing the chimneys of the Lao Brickworks. (A stupa is a Buddhist shrine.)

First impressions are important but, because they can and usually do get adjusted quite quickly, should not be allowed to form the basis of your opinion about a country. A certain amount of red tape must be endured before you are permitted to enter the country which can convey an impression of inhospitality, for example. Nothing, you will soon discover, could be further from the truth. Arrivees at Wat Tay airport in Vientiane often find themselves plunged into a chaos that appears to border on hostility. The milling, invariably good natured crowds at the airport are usually waiting to meet tourists, business people, or relatives and friends returning to Laos, in many cases, after an absence of many years. The scene, if you know how to read it, need alarm no one. Similarly, the Lao pilot I once saw on a trip upcountry, making his way from the plane to the arrivals shed with a large fish in one hand and a revolver in the other must have been a bizarre sight indeed for the uninitiated. Guns are always carried in the flight cabins and, as for the fish, well, it was probably what he brought his wife back from the wet market in Vientiane every Friday afternoon! And it certainly didn't detract from the considerable flying skills he had just demonstrated a few minutes before in making a near perfect landing on a remote, mist-shrouded airstrip. The point of course, is that appearances can be deceptive, and never more so than when you are abroad.

HEAT ON THE STREET

At least with the weather you know where you stand. Although the temperature can get up to 40°C and beyond during the drawn out days of March and April, the heat will only be withering if you overdo it or put yourself in the direct line of fire. Don't follow the example of all those monks you see, blithely sitting out in the open while the sun drums down on their shaved heads. Lao women especially, rarely expose themselves in this way and although many work out in the fields, they are admired by other Asian women for their fair skin. Those broad-brimmed, conical shaped hats that speak instantly of Indo-China exist for a purpose, and you rarely see people walking around bareheaded at noon. Foreigners with light complexions should not hesitate or feel self-conscious about applying generous layers of sun block lotion, wearing a good straw hat or to be seen scuttling into the shade for protection. A lot of Asians think they are immune to ultraviolet light, a dangerous delusion.

It may be asking a lot from foreigners who come from cooler or more easily regulated climes, but you should make an effort to adapt to the heat. People who are over dependent on air-conditioning can have a miserable time of it if they expect to be able to go from one perfect micro-climate to another. A ceiling or bedside fan will be a lot better for you in the long run.

When it's hot, it's hot: equally, when it rains, it rains. And with a vengeance! Funnily enough, you don't often see Lao people soaked to the skin during these torrents. At the slightest hint of rain, streets instantly clear of people or little handkerchief sized vinyl raincoats magically appear, conclusive proof of how well organised or well adjusted these people are to their own environment. It's mostly foreigners who seem to get caught out and it isn't uncommon to see one sprinting like a drowned rat for the cover of the nearest banyan tree or shop door!

MOVING AROUND TOWN

Various modes of transport exist in the capital and in other smaller cities. The variety can be quite bemusing at times. Within a space of a few minutes you can find yourself stepping out of an ancient, reserviced Russian helicopter that has no right to really be in the air, into the latest power-steered, all mod-cons limousine. In some remote towns like Luang Namphta in the far northwest, you can even hire a tractor to take you around. It's quite normal in fact.

Lets start our exploration of the street from the bottom up, with feet.

49

A Pedestrian View Of Town

Unless you have to rush to a business meeting or would like to turn up for your lunch appointment or bridge session looking immaculate, walking is the logical way to get around town. Its also of course, the best way to feel the pulse of the city and to acquaint yourself with its nooks and crannies, and the goings on and quotidian affairs that make up its inner life. You won't be able to catch that notice in the window of the mini-mart for a second-hand car, baby sitter or Lao tutor, for example, if you drive everywhere.

In some ways Vientiane is a city made for pedestrians. Straight, uncongested roads, generous pavements and pleasant, tree-lined riverine promenades make the going easy, except on very hot or dusty days. Be warned though, dust can be a problem, not just in the street but also at home, especially during the dry season when the level of the river drops, sand banks resurface and even the lightest breeze can turn the air into little swirling siroccos.

While you are unlikely to get trampled underfoot walking Vientiane's uncluttered streets, you might quite easily sprain your ankle. Lopsided paving stones, broken culverts and spaces that appear in front of your feet like sink holes or trap doors into the sewers, can be hazardous. Residents develop a sixth sense for such things but new arrivees should, quite literally, watch their step.

Generally though, city streets are well suited for walkers, although you need a sturdy pair of shoes. Even at night the streets are usually quite safe. Street and other forms of crime do exist but the incidence and gravity of felonies is generally quite low. An urban murder mystery would be quite a sensation indeed! Although serious crimes are not unknown, petty theft in the order of bicycle stealing are more like it. The locking-hubs from 4-wheel drives are one mysterious target for thieves. One very real danger foreigners should be aware of are attacks on vehicles by bandits. The stretch of Route 13 from Kasi to Luang Prabang is especially notorious, but residents are advised not to drive long distances at night unless they really have to. Several incidents have occurred in recent years to confirm that former anti-government rebels operating from mountain and jungle hideaways, still pose a problem.

Should you be the unlucky victim of urban crime or party to a road accident, you can easily contact one of the policemen stationed in security boxes around town. It is often more effective to make direct contact with someone like this than trying to explain the situation on the telephone. With more serious investigations involving questioning of suspects, fingerprinting, witness testimonials and so on, your local District Police Office will contact Central Police for more expert assistance. Personal contact, as with most things in Laos, usually leads to quicker results. In rural areas for example, foreigners have found that often the best way to retrieve a stolen object is to approach the local headman or village elder directly and offer a reward for its return. Expatriates living in houses in residential areas rather than apartments sometimes employ, more for peace of mind than absolute necessity, the services of a security guard. Gardeners are often happy to earn a bit extra by taking on this post.

Pineapples, pomelos and custard apple are among the fruits being sold by this cheerful Vientiane street vendor.

51

A Potpourri Of Vehicles

Finding transport around large towns and their environs is relatively easy. Apart from a five mile stretch of commercial track, long cannibalised by the resourceful Lao, that once connected Don Ket and Dong Kong island in the south, Laos has never possessed a railway network and is unlikely to for some time to come. Roads and rivers are the main arteries, with Vientiane at the centre of the main transport hub.

Buses are the kings of the road here for long distance travel or routes around the outskirts of the capital. These start at the Bus Terminal at the Talay Sao where you will find a timetable in English and Lao telling you about departure times and destinations. Buses normally leave and arrive pretty much on time, all being well that is, with punctures, broken axles, flash floods and time spent trying to wedge in half a dozen new passengers and their assorted livestock! You won't, by the way, see any designated bus stops along the way, even in Vientiane. You are expected to flag down the bus when you see it. In the developing world everything, it seems, is negotiable, even a bus, and for big groups you can easily rent at a very reasonable rate, an air-conditioned one with driver straight from the State Bus Company.

For such a small capital, Vientiane is surprisingly well serviced with all sorts of private transport to suit most needs and budgets. Prices for foreigners are almost always higher, something you will have to resign yourself to. It's sometimes difficult but there is no point in becoming indignant because, as a resident, you expect quite reasonably, to be charged the local rate. It won't happen, unless that is your Lao is fluent enough to make a convincing case for yourself.

For short distances samlors, a kind of bicycle rickshaw or *cyclo* , are good. Jumbos, three-wheeled, motor powered vehicles with side seats along the back, are next up in size. Then its the larger *tuk-tuk*, an idea imported from Thailand. Tuk-tuks resemble jumbos but are bigger and will often pick up other passengers along the way. You can get a good feel for daily life riding one of these. Unmetred taxis, usually quite old, are common but since the opening of the Friendship Bridge, air-conditioned, metred taxis have begun to appear. If you have a string of business appointments or social engagements, taxis can be hired for around US$45 a day. Make sure there are no extra surcharges for petrol or longer distances and that the car is properly insured. Transport at night is more scarce and you can easily end up paying two or three times more.

Bicycles and motorbikes – usually the 50cc type – can be hired from garages and private rental shops. There are always interesting, ergo hazardous, distractions so make sure to wear a helmet. Traffic is extremely erratic, though not usually lethal, but with more vehicles appearing every day, unpredictable road surfaces and the absence of international standards of driving, it is advisable to proceed with caution. If you should meet a convoy of police motorcycles with their sirens blaring, it usually indicates a cavalcade of dignitaries passing through. You should always stop immediately and pull into the kerb.

STREET NAMES: AN ANALOG OF HISTORY

Although street signs, both in Lao and English, are gradually appearing, monuments, temples and other landmarks continue to be referred to when explaining an address. Expatriates are in the habit of giving equivalent directions by citing buildings pertinent to the world in which they move, such as "near the American embassy," "next to the Phimphone Minimart" or "on the road to the Australian Club."

Its a form of nationalism common to many countries to name streets after heroes, poets, scientists or famous battles. The outstanding figures – the country's nation builders – in many cases, are its monarchs, and in Vientiane in particular, a stroll through its well laid out streets provides a neat analog of history. A street dedicated to Khoun Borom, the legendary king who descended to earth mounted on "a white elephant with beautiful black lips and eyelids with curved transparent tusks" and was the instrument for the country's best known creation myth, starts off the chronology. Quai Fa Ngum, named after the founder of Lane Xang, runs along the river where the large Lane Xang Hotel, the country's first international style hotel, can be found. Setthathirat and Thanon Samsenthai, both named after important rulers, complete Vientiane's three main parallel streets. Chao Anou, a monarch whose reign was short but full of tragic significance for the Lao, gets a small, cafe lined street off Setthathirat Road named after him. All these monarchs are known for their fierce sense of nationalism. You certainly won't find any streets in Laos with names like the rue August Pavie, or the Avenue Victor Hugo! A sympathetic appreciation of their national heroes will endear you to your new Lao friends and impress them with the fact that you have gone to the bother of inquiring into their history.

LIFE AL FRESCO

In comparison with the rumbustious plurality, ambition and drive that characterises many other Southeast Asian capitals, Vientiane may seem rather tame. There are few street hustlers of the Bangkok or Manila breed, although samlor drivers may gently accost you for a fare or money exchange deal. Beggars are still a relatively rare sight, and for a full two hours – more sometimes – from noon onwards, the city consigns itself to a siesta as inviolable as in any village in Andalucia. Don't be surprised if you are stopped at this hour by a tourist who has just arrived and asked if this is really the capital!

When it's not raining cats and dogs or blowing up a dust storm however, the street is where much of Lao life is conducted. In an almost silent ritual the streets blossom with colour and ceremony each morning at dawn as rows of orange and saffron-clad bonzes (Buddhist priests) converge with lines of women, many dressed in vivid silk or cotton *pha sin* skirts, who congregate to offer alms. At this hour, with cocks clearing their throats and only a few itinerant pushers of ambulants or deliverers of the morning produce to the central market in sight, the street is still the domain of the pedestrian, you could be forgiven for thinking that you are in a large country village.

The atmosphere is purposeful but rarely frantic. You seldom see any great bottlenecks on the road or jammed pavements, except for a build up of motorbikes and large numbers of school children off to an early start for classes in the tropics. With the smell of steamed rice, noodles, freshly baked baguettes and roasted coffee from street stalls and open-fronted restaurants and stores doubling as breakfast venues, you know the day is well and truly under way.

Pavements are common property and readily requisitioned by the flower or ice cream vendor, the man barbecuing succulent tidbits of chicken over a charcoal brazier, or the barbers who hang their mirrors on large tree boughs. They also serve, without too many objections being raised, as venues for the family breakfast, space for livestock, provisional altars for little clusters of incense, frangipani or yellow

A typical all-purpose general store in Paksone.

55

candles, playgrounds for toddlers and countless other uses and extensions of living rooms, kitchens and paddocks.

Wherever there is space and people there will be food. Wherever people gather, such as morning markets, bus terminals and river banks, you will find open and covered stalls. Shopping is hungry business; day and night markets also attract their fare share of food vendors. Take your own tissues if you are fussy about sticky or greasy fingers. However good you might think the food is, don't expect to be offered paper napkins after the meal!

Steaming, bubbling, piquant, and frequently unrecognisable concoctions tempt and bewilder the uninitiated. You'll soon acquaint yourself with the various foods on display but in the beginning the only way to find out if that dish is beef or sliced water-buffalo, is to try it. In some cases you may wish to know a little more about the process that went into making those fish eggs wrapped in banana leaf or that pig's trotter resting on a bed of bamboo shoots, before you take the plunge yourself. Even then you may have some identification problems with the actual ingredients. Unless you are an accomplished gourmet you may still be scratching your head even after you find perfectly good English translations of herbs, vegetables and condiments which are unexceptional to the Lao but which your dictionary tells you are galingale, kafir lime, kohrabi, yanang leaves and jelly mushrooms!

One advantage of these open-sided kitchens where all this preparation is conducted, is that you know exactly what is going on. Few Lao will object to you scrutinising their work, though they may feel a little shy. As a foreigner, your curiosity, approval and, best of all, ordering of the said dish, will always amuse and flatter the cook.

FOREIGN BODIES

While it is generally regarded as rude to stare at people, foreigners will inevitably find themselves the subject of a certain amount of natural curiosity, though rarely hard scrutiny. You're more likely in fact, to be sized up or singled out for attention by other foreigners always curious to know what chain of events brought you to a place like Laos. But who, exactly, are the expatriates who, in increasing numbers, are coming to live and work here?

Dominant among regional races like the Chinese, Vietnamese and a small community of Indian restaurateurs, tailors and jewellers, are the Thais. With the exception of those working in the aid and education field, most are involved in business. Among a socially well organised and visibly more conspicuous Western contingency, Australians and Swedes are well established. Many Europeans work as embassy staffers, for NGO groups or at the headquarters of bodies like the United States Development Program and UNICEF. There are many specialists and advisers working in the fields of oil and mineral prospecting, forestry and irrigation or for bilateral projects run by organisations like the Mekong River Commission. A number of enterprising Westerners, mostly Europeans, are now setting up as restaurateurs, gallery owners and tour operators. The majority of foreigners of European descent live in the eastern and southern section of Vientiane, although many single people or unmarried couples prefer to live in smaller, self-contained apartments in or near the centre of town. Very few Westerners have ever been granted permanent residence in Laos.

— *Chapter Four* —

SETTING UP HOUSE

Sewn pen kan eeng
Please make yourself at home!

Establishing yourself, and possibly a family, in a new country can be either a lot of fun or an exasperating ordeal. It's usually a combination of the two. The majority of expatriates will be coming to Laos to fulfil contracts that have taken weeks or months to be approved and can therefore, expect plenty of help from their employers who may already have earmarked their accommodation for them beforehand. Others may be completely independent operators arriving without housing allowances or the support of an employer.

Some newcomers will be given a short-list from which to select a suitable home. Recently vacated premises are likely to be the best option in a climate where the elements – mould, fungi, termites and more – can soon take over. Other people may find themselves, depending upon their personal budgets, temporarily stranded in a business suite, serviced apartment or guest house while they explore the property market on their own or with the help of newly made Lao friends or co-workers. Staying in temporary accommodation is not as irksome as it sounds with several hotels now catering for people in limbo by offering such things as 'Expatriate Packages' but living out of a suitcase can be wearing. Eating in restaurants every night and having different neighbours every two or three days can be unsettling. Soon you will wish to have a place of your own. If you are hoping to conduct business almost from the moment you arrive, it will be imperative to start cutting down on your phone, fax and refreshments bills by organising at least semi-permanent office space as soon as possible.

Gradually more properties of all kinds are beginning to appear on the rental market, the result of greater demand and more funds to restore existing buildings that have fallen into disrepair and ruin. Various types of accommodation, compatible with the needs of a career diplomat or the humble ODA worker getting by on not much more than the local salary, exist. These range from detached brick and plaster houses, small apartments on the second floor of Chinese style shop-houses, concrete blocks of the Soviet welfare variety, and restored or partly renovated French villas. If you have the time and a flair for creative design or are good at do-it-yourself, you may consider taking over a building of the kind in need of repair or conversion. Some foreigners, with the necessary time and means, have begun restoring and beautifying old homes in Vientiane to their own standards and tastes. Many surprisingly gracious homes have been created in this way.

FINDING THE RIGHT HOME

Many of the same considerations apply when looking for a house in Laos as they do in most countries but there are some local factors which you should bear in mind. The first considerations apart from the rental, will be location and size. If you are going to be living in the suburbs, remember that the rustic charm of a leafy, unmade road may wear off in the rainy season when it becomes virtually inaccessible except to 4-wheel drives or earth removers! If your house or garden is in a particularly low lying area it may be subject to flooding at this time too.

Temples add ambiance and character to an area, but remember that, because Buddhism is alive and well in Laos and temples and pagodas have always been social centres as well as religious ones, there will be a considerable amount of coming and going as well as noise, especially at festival times. If you are an early riser, the proximity of a temple will suit you to a tee as the tradition in Laos is for monks to vigorously beat drums four times a month – when the moon is in its first quarter, full, last and no moon phases – at around 4.00 a.m.! Depending how sensitive you are to public noise, loud-speakers, which transmit news, propaganda and music twice daily – in the early morning and evening – and are placed at many points throughout cities, and even in normally tranquil Mekong River villages, may be a problem. Parties and celebrations are rarely held during the rainy season because it coincides with the Buddhist Lent, but bearing in mind that the Lao do enjoy a good knees-up, don't be surprised if things start livening up when the rains clear.

Inspecting Your New Home

Part of the attraction of Lao cities is that they easily blend rural and urban characteristics. Trees, pastures, paddy and flowing shrub mix effortlessly with traffic, pedestrians and shops. The animal world all this greenery supports can be a symphony of unwelcome noise and annoyance you should bear in mind when thinking about location. Two or three roosters welcoming the dawn every day – chickens don't take Sundays off! – or the sound of bullfrogs in the paddies at night may be more piercing than you imagined. Be aware that marshy land, torpid rivers and areas near large clumps of trees are the perfect breeding grounds for mosquitoes and legions of other insects. Always check to see how much progress the insect world has made in the house you are inspecting by probing into cupboards, under carpets, standing units and in air-vents. Shake the curtains or blinds to see what is released. It is virtually impossible to keep houses insect free but some places are more susceptible than others. If a house is infested but looks structurally sound, it may just be the result of neglect or a long absence of tenants. You can ask the agency or owner to fumigate the house. It usually only takes one day to do.

When viewing accommodation, don't be shy about trying out every single tap, flush, button, window latch and faucet that you can lay your eyes on. Spluttering and rusty water, rattling pipes and soggy washers and the like are the sort of thing you will be looking out for. Check that there are adequate pumps and tanks also as some parts of Vientiane have water pressure problems, particularly upstairs bathrooms and toilets. This can sometimes last for several hours but there is no predicting when.

Make sure that electric sockets are tight-fitting, not hanging from the walls like Jack-in-the-Boxes, and that the wiring runs down a dry course wall, not parallel with, or across potentially leaky pipes. If household appliances or gadgets like toasters and fruit blenders are included in the contract, pilot run the lot. Most accommodation offered to foreigners these days will have air-conditioning, albeit

ancient units, installed in some of the rooms. Switch at least one of them on when you arrive, then you'll see if there is any significant difference in the room temperature when you come to leave. Some of the older units start to make a terrible racket after they have been running for a while.

If something is broken or not functioning properly, it can be attended to at the owner's expense or used to get a rent or deposit reduction. Carefully check the building material, their age and state. A 70-year-old home, made from teak with several of its original tiles still intact, may look charming but can prove surprisingly porous. One American lady, inspecting an elegant though rather rundown looking villa, found the empty box of a French product with the word 'Souricide' written on it in red letters. Not speaking the language herself, she looked it up in the dictionary, discovering that the word 'souri' in French meant 'mouse.' Informal inquiries among the Lao neighbours revealed that the house was overrun by a nocturnal army of rats!

Real estate agents exist to help you find accommodation. It is important to find out if there are any hidden expenses and how much the agents commission is going to come to first. You can also ask around the foreign community for available properties. Check the ads in shop windows or in expatriate clubs as well. Here is a fairly representative sample of an advertisement for a house suitable for a family, that appeared in an expatriate newsletter:

House For Rent

2 storey Lao style house: brick plastered downstairs with tile floors, wood construction upstairs with wood floors, 3 bedrooms, 2 baths, a.c. in bedrooms, fans in living area. Newly painted. Quiet location, easy access. Enclosed yard with gate. Rent negotiable.

With a map included you could have a quick peep at the place first then, if you like the look of it, phone for a rough idea of the rent figure before arranging to meet the owner. Standards vary enormously from apartments with stone sinks and exposed wiring to tastefully restored colonial villas with swimming pools and garden sprinklers. Always check at least three or four houses for the sake of comparison even if you fall in love with the first one you see. With the help of a good map, pin point the areas you would, or wouldn't, like to live in, preferably in consultation with an old Lao hand. You will want to know how the house is placed for routes to work, school, shops and other amenities.

Although you may not want to live where there is a high concentration of foreigners, it's worth reflecting that there are probably several very good reasons why certain areas have become popular with expatriates. Generally speaking, areas with a high density of foreign residents are likely to be at the more expensive end of the property market, while predominantly Lao populated districts, even in the city centre, usually turn out to be cheaper, particularly apartments. You will have to think not only about how much space you will need but also if you will require household staff, and if so, the space allowance required to accommodate them. Very few staff actually

This sensitively renovated villa in downtown Vientiane is owned by a well known American textile designer.

live in, but you will want to avoid tripping over each other's toes in the daytime. You will also have to consider how much social or business entertaining you will be doing and how many guests you can accommodate at one go. For an increasing number of expatriates working with grass roots NGO groups or volunteer organisations in Laos, considerations like these will not apply. One Australian couple who lived in Vientiane for a number of years – the husband worked for UNICEF and his wife was a nurse – managed very well on a combined income of around US$700 per month, $250 of which went on the rent of a spacious, basic but adequately equipped four-room apartment smack bang in the centre of Vientiane. You will meet many expatriates who get by on considerably less. Whatever your budget, choosing the right house will be one of the most important decisions you make. It will be your best chance of privacy, a refuge from work induced stress or the more adverse effects of culture shock.

WHAT TO BRING

Although you can find fully furnished accommodation if you try hard enough, most rentals will be unfurnished so you will be starting from scratch – buying your own basic essentials in Vientiane or Bangkok, from expatriates on the way out or from friends willing to bring items back for you from their trips in the region. Whether you arrive with just one suitcase or a mountain of boxes will depend on how generous the excess baggage allowance on your work contract is, if you have one, and the duration of your stay. There will be other dictates of course, such as the style in which you are accustomed to living.

The basic household items needed to survive any foreign posting, such as refrigerators, washing machines, and luxury goods like stereos, televisions and even karaoke sets, are readily available at the large Morning Market in Vientiane or smaller suppliers popping up around town. Bringing your own short-wave radio is recommended. In the case of electrical appliances you may need to convert plugs to the two-pin sockets used in Laos. Universal plug adapters are useful. The voltage quivers around 220 volts. Surges can be a problem with sensitive items like personal computers which can burn out. Unless your computer has a built in compensator you will need a surge protector. All important equipment should be grounded.

Colour coordinating your own personal possessions or locally bought pieces of furniture with curtains, carpets, bed covers and the like has become much easier with the recent revival of the Lao textile industry and some excellent innovations in the design and colour, not only of traditional and ceremonial clothing, but of wall hangings, coveralls, cushion cases, table cloths and fashionable upholstery fabrics. Other household items of high aesthetic quality may be hard to find and you may have to rely upon your trips outside the country or through mail order companies to obtain good quality cutlery, and the fittings and fixtures to suit your own tastes. Items that some people consider indispensable like microwave ovens and percolators turn up from time to time but you shouldn't rely on shops having them in stock when you want them. If you see something you like, grab it while you can!

Linen is available locally but most people prefer to bring their own, at least sheets and pillow cases. Towels and bath mats should not be too thick as drying them during the rainy season can be a headache. Bring your own pillows if you are a light sleeper: the local ones, made from kapok and compacted foam, may be too hard for you. Utensils made from cheap alloy tend to bend and droop under pressure. Its a good idea to bring your own dishes, pots and pans, knives and forks, kettles and cork screws if you want to have things that last. You don't have to go all the way to Bangkok to find good kitchen utensils. You can find all of these things in Udon Thani, the nearest commercial Thai city of any size to Vientiane.

If there are any favourite food goodies you would be loath to go without you should bring them along, but generally speaking most standard foods and flavourings, including a good selection of herbs, are readily available. Japanese residents will have a tougher time finding the common ingredients of their cuisine like dry *natto*, *aji no motto*, *furikaki* or more rarefied foods in Laos and should make arrangements to receive relief packages of condiments and flavourings from home.

Straightforward furniture designs can be made to your specifications from local hardwoods, rattan and bamboo. If you think this is a possibility, try to bring some furniture catalogues with you.

If you have children, try to anticipate their needs well in advance. You will be so busy yourself during the first few weeks in Laos that it is easy to overlook children or not to notice that they have grown one size bigger since you left home. Apart from clothing, there are even more important considerations regarding children. While the combination of living and attending school abroad may seem like the perfect preparation for life in the global village, culture shock and childhood make unpredictable partners. Make sure you bring along at least a few of their personal possessions like books, toys or favourite videos to help them through the transition. If you wish to give your children good quality presents for Christmas and birthdays it might be wise to obtain these in advance.

Good baby food is quite difficult to find. You might consider bringing a food processor to make your own. This is not as difficult as it sounds as infant formulas are sold in most markets and mini-marts. Nappy rash medications, creams and cotton diapers are difficult to come by, though expensive, disposable diapers are readily available.

CLOTHING

In the matter of clothing, dress for the tropics with the expectation of a cool November–January season requiring sweaters and light jackets. Expatriates in Vientiane can enjoy a full social life if they so wish but, unless they are on the diplomatic circuit, formal wear is not needed, smart casual being the norm for most invitations. Men should bring at least one suit with them however, for the occasional semi-formal function. A spare safari suit is useful but usually implies an outdoor setting. Plenty of spare cotton underwear is recommended as these items tend to have a short life in the tropics.

Women in particular may find that clothes which hardly raised an eyebrow in the streets of New York, Stockholm or Tokyo look conspicuously out of place in Laos. See-through blouses, bare shoulders, plunging necklines and ultra short skirts and shorts fall into the category of immodest wear. The Lao are far too polite to publicly condemn what they privately view as an immodestly dressed women or disrespectfully attired man but it will be quietly noted and remarked upon out of earshot. Let common sense and a close observation of local standards be your guide. Foreign women report that when they turn up for social events and special functions dressed in traditional Lao clothing – the wraparound skirt called *pha sin* and the *pha biang* – a matching silk shawl – this is much appreciated by the Lao.

The garments industry is one of Laos's largest export sectors these days but, especially if you are a stickler for fashion, you might prefer shopping for clothes in Bangkok. This also applies if you are a large person by Lao standards. Good leather shoes in larger sizes are difficult to find. Footwear is important as shoes tend to wear out quickly because of rough surfaces, mud and rain. There are many tailors in Vientiane. While most of their work is of a rather practical kind, following rather traditional designs for women, they are dexterous at copying cutouts from magazines or even rough sketches. You may have to supply some of the haberdashery (zips, buttons, buckles etc.) yourself if you want the right finishing. Husbands should be warmed that women who find the right tailor with a good feel for their design needs have been known to commission entire spring or summer collections at one go!

HOUSEHOLD GENIES

If you rent a house which has formerly had a Lao tenant or owner you may inherit a spirit house or, more likely, a small niche, shelf or other enclave serving as a modest Buddhist altar. These may also be located in the garden as they more frequently are in Thailand and Myanmar, at the spot where a tree has been cut down and the resident spirit provided with quick alternative accommodation. Niches set aside for spirits or religious offerings are not specific to one particular spot in or near the house though they are in some cultures like the Chinese, where almost every house or restaurant – even McDonald's in Hong Kong – have their own altars to the kitchen god sitting on a little wall bracket.

Here is a good opportunity to demonstrate your respect for the local culture. As the new householder you should try to maintain the custom of making regular offerings of rice, fruit, flowers and incense, a duty which, if you have domestic staff, they will feel very comfortable discharging. Contributing financially to any visits undertaken and offerings made by members of your staff to the local temple will be much appreciated. Whatever your private thoughts or religious convictions are about such things, it goes without saying that you should never openly ridicule or belittle other people's beliefs however implausible they may sound to you. Showing respect and interest in such matters will not only earn you a bit of merit in the Buddhist sense, but also endear you to your Lao neighbours.

DOMESTIC HELP

When the French ran Indo-China it seemed that you needed a different servant to perform every conceivable household function. Those days are long gone but the tradition of foreigners employing domestic staff lingers on, partly from considerations of space, time and know-how but also perhaps, because the lifestyle and climate of Laos in particular and Southeast Asia in general, is conducive to employing staff to do what you would normally be quite resigned to undertake yourself. It just goes to show how different the tropics are from the countries of the northern hemisphere.

You don't need legions of servants to run a tight ship. A good half of expatriate households in Laos employ some kind of domestic help, even if it's only an all-purpose cooking, shopping, cleaning, child minding person. You will soon find out how dependent you need or want to be on outside help or how feasible it is to run the entire show on your own.

Many foreign women, unaccustomed to dealing with hired staff will have to first overcome a sense of discomfort, even guilt, at the thought of delegating hitherto perfectly normal household chores to strangers. By employing domestic staff you are not only supporting the local economy and helping a Lao person to improve their own family's standard of living, but also creating the perfect opportunity to interact with a native person and to learn Lao ways first hand. Most foreign residents who can justify the expense and commitment, opt to have some form of household help. Apart from the obvious benefits of cutting down or eliminating irksome chores, it will allow you more free time to organise your new life in Laos, to take up all those interests and hobbies you never seemed to get around to before and to engage more fully in the community you are now a part of. Here is the chance for a well earned respite. After a lifetime of household duties, you deserve it.

Finding the Right Person

The majority of Lao are honest and averagely diligent people, but no one is infallible and only time will tell whether you can depend 100% on the staff you employ. Apart from the obvious considerations of capability the most important thing is that you hit it off with your staff. First instincts often prove to be right but if the person you are thinking of taking on has a track record of reliable service within the foreign community, this can be very reassuring in a country where references are almost unheard of. This is where personal or third person recommendations can be useful. You might be lucky and be able to take on someone coming to the end of their service with a departing family, an arrangement good for both parties. Friends may be able to ask their own domestic staff to recommend a relative or friend for a post or to put the word out on the network that you require help. As long as this is not being done simply to discharge a debt towards somebody, you should be able to find people with a certain seal of approval, although of course, there are no such things as guarantees when it comes down to people. An element of trust is always required when accepting other people's recommendations.

Accessing your own national group can often work well. Members of the Swedish community in Laos for example, are well known for going to great lengths to make sure their staff are not left in the limbo of unemployment by setting them up with work wherever possible, in the houses of their compatriots. The Japanese, with their very particular food needs and highly developed networking, often do the same. Community associations, clubs and newsletters provide free exposure for your needs. You can also put adverts in the local mini-marts frequented by foreigners and their staff or in the English language *Vientiane Times*, or the French monthly *Le Mekong*. It is usually safe enough to put your name and telephone number. The Ministry of Foreign Affairs are more than happy to inquire on your behalf about staff. They may even be able to put you in contact with staff who speak or have some working knowledge of English, French, Swedish, or Japanese.

Interviewing Prospective Members of Staff

How good are you at character assessment? If you have done this sort of thing before, your experiences will stand you in good stead for this difficult task. If not, take a deep breath and read on!

You should consult with other residents in any case, to find out what sort of questions you need to ask. First of course, you must decide how many members of staff you require. Then make a detailed list of what duties you will expect from them, a checklist that you will have to produce at the interview. If you intend to employ an extensive staff you may need help from a more experienced person at this stage. Remember that you will be looking for staff who can get on well with each other so compatibility of personality will be an important consideration when putting together a team. If the staff get on well together they will be able to sort out a lot of their own problems without burdening you.

At the interview stage try and find out as much as you can about the person's background. Nobody will resent you asking them how old they are, their marital status, if they have brought up children of their own, if their parents are still alive – you will need the address of at least one close relative in the event of illness – previous experience, distance from work and literacy levels. As you will not be reasonably expected to speak much Lao at this stage, the interview will be a good chance to evaluate the person's language skills.

Staff rarely live-in in Laos but you might like to know which meals, if any, they will be taking at your home, and which days they will be having off. You should familiarise yourself with the Lao national holidays so that you can anticipate being staffless on those days. Check in advance how many days they will expect to be off for events like the Lao Pi Mai (New Year) festival or special days like Christmas and Chinese holidays if these apply.

On the question of salary it is best to stick to the accepted average, paying any small bonuses or supplements if and when you deem the time right. A survey carried out by the Women's International Group for 1996/7, suggested the following average monthly rates of pay – according to experience – for staff employed by foreigners. (Amounts are in US dollars.)

- Cook or Chef   130–220
- Cook Maid   100–140
- Maid   100–140
- Baby Minder   100–140
- Nanny   100–120
- Gardener   100–120
- Watchman   100–120
- Driver   150–200

There may be some overlap between jobs. Gardeners for example, often act as security guards and general Mr. Fixits.

Staying Within the Law

Employees are protected by the law and before you hire someone in Laos a written contract, available from the Ministry of Labour, must be signed. The form sets out a minimum wage of 26,000 kip per month and stipulates the conditions for overtime rates which vary according to day and night-time hours, and arrangements made for periods during official holidays and work during agreed days off.

If you wish to terminate a contract, notice must be given 45 days in advance. One important consideration to note is that on completion of a contract employers are required to pay a bonus equal to 10% of the total salary paid to the employee during his or her period of service. If a member of staff has been with you for over three years, the rate goes up to 15%. Contracts, if breached, can be terminated without compensation.

So-called 'industrial accidents' are a serious matter in Laos. If an accident occurs to one of your employees either at work or on the way to work, you are liable to pay his or her full salary for a full six months if they are incapacitated. Half the workers wages must be paid for the next 18 months. Should you leave Laos beforehand, the remaining balance must be paid before departure. Members of staff for their part, must produce a doctor's certificate when taking leave for medical reasons. It is generally accepted that employers bear an unwritten responsibility for the health and welfare of their staff. This may require among other things, helping out with medical fees and treatment which most Lao cannot afford to pay for themselves. Although the choice of companies is rather limited at the moment, it is not a bad idea getting insurance cover for your staff.

Getting On With Staff

While maintaining the boss–worker relationship to some extent, always treat your staff as equals. Remember that this is a country which fought long and hard to free itself from foreign domination and to replace hierarchical systems of rank with a more egalitarian way of doing things. You don't have to be a devil – dragons are well thought of in Indo-China – to run your household staff efficiently. Most Lao workers are quietly methodical and unobtrusive. Half the time you probably won't even be aware that they are around.

Once basic rules have been established don't assume that your Lao staff will strictly abide by them. Reinforce your requests or it may be assumed that you only required something to be done once. If a chore is not carried out properly, go patiently through the whole procedure again. A show of anger or petulance will not get you very far in Laos and may eventually result in the defection of staff you have spent valuable time training. If you need to tell a member of staff in no uncertain terms to pull their socks up, always do it in private, never in front of other Lao, otherwise the person being reprimanded will lose face with their peers. Never single out members of staff for public criticism. If you need to convey dissatisfaction in a group situation, address the problem in a general manner.

Remember that your staff are not mind readers. Be very explicit about your requirements. Set down your needs from the outset and make sure that they are properly attended to. Every household is run differently and duties vary considerably. Don't assume that your maid will know how or when to defrost the freezer, change the vacuum bag, or how to fit the filters into your percolator. Be very particular about hygiene , how you wish food to be prepared and how you would like your accounts and money receipts kept.

You may have to accompany a maid on some of her early shopping trips although you should make it quite clear that it is she not you, who is buying. In fruit, vegetable and wet markets there are often two prices: one for the Lao and another for foreigners. No prizes for guessing who pays more! If there are any special Lao dishes that you would like to eat at home, jot the names down and get your maid or cook to prepare them for you. There is only one Lao cookbook available in print at the moment but you can show your staff pictures of Thai dishes which are often quite similar and let them experiment.

Once lunch has been served, don't expect your staff to be very frisky for a couple of hours. The Lao siesta is an institution. Don't be surprised or concerned if you see staff stretched out on the cool floor tiles of your entrance hall or kitchen at this time. Its quite normal. I recall entering the children's wing of the Bibliotech Nationale at noon one day only to find the entire staff in a deep slumber in one big, convivial heap on the floor!

The relationship you have with your staff will be one of the key factors in determining the enjoyment and success of your stay in Laos and one of the strongest memories of the country you will cherish in the future. Finally, remember that very few Lao have only ever had contact with foreigners and will know very little about foreign customs and habits. The onus is on you to learn as much as you can about Lao culture and life.

SURVIVING WITHOUT HELP

Many people do, especially single expatriates on meagre ODA salaries, young people, couples without children, or those who simply prefer to do things their own way or to enjoy as much privacy as possible when they can. Many people, particularly in the aid and development field, find themselves upcountry for long, sometimes unpredictable periods at a stretch, during which their homes are left untenanted.

If a sink needs unblocking or a fuse box reinstalling, there are plenty of shops that can help out, although if you are living upcountry you will probably have to find one of those gifted odd-job men that most rural towns or villages have. There are also a small number of contractors happy to do a bit of cleaning, gardening and general maintenance on request. Evening or night markets allow people to do their shopping after work and the number of options for eating out are steadily increasing and improving. There are even take away and home delivery services in the capital.

Single women's privacy is usually respected and it is generally quite safe for them to live alone. If you make an effort to cultivate good relations with your neighbours they can help to keep an eye on the place while you are absent. Such things as nuisance calls are still rare in this conservative country and have certainly not reached the levels they have elsewhere.

DEALING WITH MONEY AND BILLS

Foreigners who lived here in the late 1980s and early 1990s, recount horrendous delays and hassles trying to conduct even the simplest banking transaction. Mercifully, things have improved considerably

75

since those days. The banking system has benefited in the last few years from increasing competitiveness resulting from the advent of foreign banks and the general stimulus of the country's sweeping economic reforms. At the present count there are eight state owned commercial banks, two joint-venture banks and six Thai branches.

Foreigners are welcome to open accounts in US dollars, Thai baht or Lao kip. Interest at standard international rates is paid on foreign currency deposit accounts. Shopkeepers have not started adding their own unofficial commissions onto the purchase price of goods paid for with credit cards yet, as they have in other countries in this region. Cheque books are issued to new clients and a small charge made for cash withdrawals. As this varies between banks you should find out what the commission is before you open your account.

Travellers cheques are gaining recognition with their wider use and can be cashed at all commercial banks or at any of the several foreign exchange bureaus licensed by the Bank of Lao PDR which can be found in most major towns and at an increasing number of hotels, restaurants and even in some shops these days. Transactions are usually conducted in an honest, though time consuming manner.

Air tickets obtained at Lao Aviation counters or through travel agents can be paid with Visa cards or foreign currency. The agent for Visa in Laos is the Banque pour le Commerce Exterieur du Lao (BCEL). They have a cash withdrawal service here. Several commercial banks are able to deal with international transfers.

Financial transactions outside of large towns are quite a different story. Be prepared to pack large bundles of cash when travelling upcountry or, if stationed in remote areas, arrange for money to be transferred to a Lao bank in the nearest town of any size. In many instances this is easier said than done as volunteer workers, engineers, agronomists and the like may find themselves way out in the boon docks for weeks at a time in villages barely on the periphery of the cash economy themselves.

The Currency

The kip is the official currency of Laos. Denominations are 1000, 500, 100, 50, 20, 10, 5, and 1. Coins and notes of small value are gradually being withdrawn from circulation. Although US dollars and Thai baht are officially banned for domestic transactions, they are freely used in the marketplace. It is quite normal to pay and be dibbed out your change in a shop in a bewildering welter of coins and notes in three different currencies. If you are not good at converting figures in your head, carry a pocket calculator with you on shopping excursions. Officially kip cannot be taken out of the country. There is no earthly reason why you would want to anyway, except perhaps to show curious friends back home, as the currency has no trading value on the international monetary market. There is a negligible difference these days between the official bank exchange rate and what you can expect to receive on the black market.

Business hours in Laos vary according to the seasons, or more specifically the temperature, offices and banks generally opening from 7.30 to 11.30 a.m. and 2.00 to 5.00 p.m. during the hot months, and from 8.00 to 12.00 a.m. and 2.00 to 5.00 p.m. during the cooler months from November to February. Many offices open on Saturday mornings. Banks are among the only businesses that stay open during the long, soporific noon siesta, but there are lots of exceptions to this pattern so always check opening hours beforehand.

LA POSTE

All things considered the postal system in Laos is a reasonably efficient and reliable one. No one though, would say that it is a fast service. You should allow between 10 to 14 days on average for mail to arrive safely at its destination. In the case of valuable or urgent mail it is better to forward it EMS or by courier service, both tried and tested methods. If mail becomes lost, as occasionally happens, it is usually because of illegible addressing or a sorting problem, rarely because of dishonesty. The Lao postal service is inexpensive.

The General Post Office (La Poste General) just opposite the large Morning Market in Vientiane, also has a number of public telephone cabins for making local, national and international calls. The GPO is also where you pay your bills. The Post Office is open from Monday to Saturday. A counter for sending letters stays open during lunch. You can also collect your mail at this time. Newcomers have been known to wait weeks for the postman to turn up with the first eagerly awaited batch of letters from home, only to find that normal mail delivery services in Laos do not exist. The post is collected from allocated boxes at the GPO. You will be given a box for a small rental fee plus a down payment of 1600 kip. You can check your box for incoming mail from Monday to Saturday, from 7.30 to 17.00, or 8.00 to 18.00 during the winter. If you have received larger parcels or packages, you will find a note to that effect in your box. In the case of EMS mail you will be told by telephone. Postal workers occasionally neglect to notify people so if you are expecting a parcel that doesn't appear to have arrived, you should make inquiries.

Censorship is still practised in Laos although nobody seems to be quite sure how rigorously. Most letters arrive unopened, but all incoming parcels and packets are subject to inspection by customs officials. Outgoing mail is less frequently checked. Most mail will be placed in the domestic and overseas letter boxes outside the GPOs, although a number of impressive orange mail boxes have begun to appear on the streets of Vientiane recently. No one seems quite sure how often the mail is collected from them though!

Your correspondents abroad are recommended to use the official title of the country – LAO PDR – in preference to simply 'Laos.' To avoid the inevitable furrowed eyebrows and scratching of heads among the postal staff at home, you could advise them to add 'Southeast Asia' after the above designation.

TELEPHONES AND TELECOMMUNICATIONS

Until as recently as 1990, Laos was connected to the outside world by only one line, with the exception of links to Thailand and the Soviet Union. Callers would have to patiently wait up to two or three hours to place a call, as only one subscriber could ring at any one time. Things have come a long way since then. World Bank funding and Japanese aid have combined to create a state-of-the-art digital telephone exchange providing international connections via satellite links to Hong Kong, Japan and Australia. A fibre optic network connects the main exchange to subordinate ones in remoter areas like Thakhek, Paksan and Luang Prabang. The new telephone system is certainly modern and efficient but there are limitations and many provincial towns lag behind.

Demand has risen with the improvements and in some parts of Vientiane, particularly the commercial centre, you may have to put your name on a waiting list in order to get connected. Generally, getting a line installed is a straight forward enough procedure. You should go in person to the Enterprise Telecommunication Laos (ELT) office with your passport and apply. You will have to sign a contract

if you need to have an IDD connection. Depending upon the capacity of the area in which you live it will take from three to four weeks before you are serviced. This should be taken as a minimum figure. Longer waits are quite routine. You will have to pay three fees: for connection, the telephone apparatus and cable respectively. Telephone bills are paid at the GPO.

Long distance domestic calls are assessed on distance, most calls falling into the 200–300 kip per minute range. Like IDD tariffs, you will be expected to pay the next minute count if you overrun. This means that, if you had made a 2 minute and 15 second call, you would be charged for a full 3 minutes.

ELT also runs a telephone and fax service which is open daily from 8.00 a.m. until 10.00 p.m. Rates on domestic and international calls are charged at the standard rate. Mobile phones can also be used. Some of the larger hotels have fax and IDD services available to the public. The original single cell, analog service is not recommended as it is subject to frequent breakdowns. The more recent multiple cell GMS digital system suffers far less system failures, its quality is higher and its coverage wider. The system cannot be used outside of Vientiane province at present but there are plans to make it nationwide and also to include roaming to Thailand. Likewise, paging services at present are limited to Vientiane and you are required to be a Lao speaker in order to leave messages on the network.

If you need to install a modem to access the Internet and e-mail services, you should check the quality of your wiring to your nearest exchange to make sure it is up to scratch. Otherwise there are few problems involved in data transfer of this kind.

ELECTRICITY

The electric current in Laos is relatively high: 220 volts, with variation due to frequent fluctuations. Two-pin sockets are standard here so you might have to bring an adapter or step-up transformer with you. Voltage regulators and surge suppressers are recommended for sensitive equipment such as computers or high definition televisions. These should be earthed. Most wiring is not grounded and often the safety standards leave a lot to be desired. If the wiring is clearly dangerous – you may have to consider the safety of young children – get the owner to do something about it before you move into the house. If you end up footing the bill yourself it can turn out to be very expensive. Extreme caution should be applied when dealing with wiring and contact between wet or damp surfaces and electrical parts avoided at all cost.

Although the supply of electrical power from province to province is uneven, the country's enormous hydroelectric potential has meant a steady improvement in the supply of electricity to rural areas. Blackouts still occur, even in Vientiane, so a good stock of candles, an oil or kerosene lamp, matches and a torch, all kept somewhere you can easily locate them in the dark, is advisable. Bills are paid at the offices of the ELD (Electricite du Laos). If you prefer, you can also pay your bill directly to the ELD person who delivers it.

WATER

Generally, the supply of water in major towns is good, although it is not recommended to drink it unless it has been boiled for a minimum of 15–20 minutes. Fixing a filter to the tap also helps to eliminate impurities. Most people stick to mineral water.

Always check where the water pipes have been installed and whether there is any visible leakage. Moisture is the bane of the tropics and untamed water can lead to mustiness, mould and all the problems contingent with bacteria supporting organisms of this kind. You need to watch out for drops in water pressure which usually occur because of problems of altitude rather than supply. Water shortages during the dry season are not uncommon. Foreigners pay more for their water than the Lao! Different rates also apply to offices, factories and so on. *Bo phen ngan*, as they say in Laos – "It can't be helped" or, "There's not much you can do about it!"

In Vientiane, bills can be paid at the central Lao Water Supply Office on Thanon Phon Kheng or, as with your telephone bills, to the person presenting you with them.

SHOPPING AND PERSONAL SERVICES

With the rapid development of Vientiane as one of the emerging commercial centres of the lower Mekong region, many new shops have sprung up to cater for a resident population whose ranks are gradually being swollen by rural migrants, visiting business people and an increasingly large expatriate community whose special needs, tastes and relative affluence have stimulated the market place and created some quite sophisticated shopping opportunities.

Basically, there are three types of shopping venues. Individual establishments like bakeries, tailors, photo stores, jewellery and flower shops; general stores which, like French epicerie, sell all sorts of edibles and domestic items; mini-marts which sell the same kind of thing but also tend to stock imported goodies and delicatessen style goods. They occasionally also sell foreign newspapers, magazines and newsletters produced for the foreign community. The third and largest shopping forum is the market.

Talad, or markets, are the best places for general shopping and are a fascinating showcase for the country's products. You will need to visit the so-called Morning Market in Vientiane – it actually opens until the evening – several times to familiarise yourself with its labyrinthine inner passages. Markets are usually divided into what you might call dry and wet produce. The first stock everything from electronics and cosmetics to sacks of charcoal and crates of Tiger Beer; the wet market is where you will shop for fish, meat, fruit and vegetables, herbs, condiments and flowers. The produce is best bought before noon as fish and meat is not refrigerated, though it may sometimes be displayed on blocks of ice. Market food is usually of excellent quality. Don't hesitate to pick up, squeeze and prod the merchandise. Everybody does it.

In country towns the best of the morning market may be over as early as 10 o'clock. Bartering is the norm for most goods on sale in the markets. If you have Lao employees they will almost certainly be able to buy all the food you need from here at a fraction of the price it would cost you. If you do end up shopping regularly for yourself, shadow other customers – Lao naturally – and see what they pay for their half kilo of artichokes or Mekong carp, and then put in the same bid for the identical item. It is advisable to become adept at the Lao counting system as quickly as possible.

Dairy products are almost always imported, and things like milk are best bought in sterilised, refrigerator cooled packets. Thanks to the French influence, fresh baguettes are widely available in larger towns, and can usually be picked up at roadside stalls or from ambulants placed outside the morning markets, bus terminals, schools and other public buildings. *Pate kao jii*, a sandwich made from luncheon meat, is a popular stand-up breakfast or take away.

Shopping hours tend to be arbitrary but most places will be open from about 8 o'clock in the morning until 7 or 8 in the evening. If you want to be served at lunch time you may have to clear your throat a couple of times to rouse the staff from their cat-naps!

Huge, Bangkok style, all purpose arcades and malls are the next step in the Vientiane shopping scene. There is already one of these joint venture monsters, or monstrosities, along Samsenthai Road.

Good Buys

Lao textiles are one of the best kept shopping secrets of Southeast Asia. Handmade products of exceptional quality can still be bought for a song. Many wily foreigners have already bought up the best antique textiles but bargains still remain. Woven silk fabric is used to create wall tapestries, wraparound skirts, wedding dresses, burial shrouds, shawls, the intricate techniques of ikat and brocade and, more recently, the knick-knacks of the tourist market like shoulder bags and cushion covers. The cornucopic Morning Market in Vientiane has the largest selection and is a good introduction to the art. There are several textile galleries and handicraft shops in Vientiane and Luang Prabang specialising in new and antique textiles. There are weaving communities on the outskirts of most large towns where you can watch women working at their looms and buy directly at a small saving.

Ready made or made to order furniture in rattan, bamboo, cane and high quality wood can be bought at low cost for use while you are in Laos and then eventually shipped home. Decoration and novelty items like mirror frames, toys, picnic baskets and lamps are easily sought out. The Lao have always excelled at woodcarving. If you like wood ornaments and statues there are many good workshops maintaining this tradition. Good quality silver jewellery in both traditional and modern designs retails at a reasonable price and is usually sold by weight. Vientiane and Luang Prabang have several well known silversmiths.

PERSONAL SERVICES

Vientiane residents won't have many problems finding shops or workshops specialising in key cutting, household appliances, video and TV repairs. Other personal services likely to be of use to foreigners include packers and shippers, photographic services, real estate offices, home and party catering, and office suppliers.

On the business and work side there are several enterprising new companies selling and servicing computer equipment and software, office equipment, automation and repair, and services like typing, word processing, photocopying, and the translation of documents and contracts. A lot of foreigners get their letter-headed papers, business cards and the like made up in Bangkok as the quality of printing in Laos still remains low though it is improving steadily.

ON THE ROAD IN LAOS

Getting started with a car in Laos is relatively easy. First however, you should think about whether you really need one. Make sure that you are not just automatically slipping into the habits of a former life in which it was mandatory to own and drive a car. Plenty of people manage without. Try surviving a month or so without a car.

If you decide that you must have wheels, the first step is to obtain a Lao driving license. You can drive for one month on an international license if you are a short term resident or tourist. Residents however, must have a Lao license to drive here. This should be applied for as soon as possible. In order to obtain this you need to take whatever license you have along to the Office of Vehicle and Driving License Control at the Ministry of Telecommunication and Construction. You'll be issued with a temporary license valid for three months after which you'll qualify for a longer one. At present there are two types: the first must be extended like a visa, in this case every two years; the second type is valid for an indefinite period. Licenses in Laos are colour coded into a number of different categories. If you are working in the commercial or private enterprise group for example, your license plate will be black, the numbers white; NGOs are designated blue and resident expatriates yellow and blue. As a further disincentive to driving in the mountain and jungle regions of Laos, be warned that cars bearing this last plate have been singled out by bandits armed to the teeth with M-16s and hand grenades. If you have never driven before, it is possible to take the driving test here in a number of different languages, but it is easier said than done.

To date I've only witnessed one truly enraged Lao driver – an elderly gentleman who was overtaken by a sneering tractor driver – who could be accused of suffering an injured machismo pride. Times are changing however, and even the long fuse of Lao patience is showing signs of shortening. The dawn of the irascible driver may be about to break. The Lao have always driven instinctively rather than by the book, but with a considerable increase in traffic volume over the last few years the unfazed but erratic style of driving that characterises the Lao approach is increasingly incompatible with the improved roads and more powerful motors that are beginning to appear on the streets of Vientiane.

Practical driving distances tend to be shorter than they are in other countries. You are unlikely to find yourself driving for example, between major Lao cities unless it is work related, in which case you will probably be using a 4-wheel drive or heavy goods vehicle for the trip. This is partly because the condition of many of these roads less travelled still leaves much to be desired, but also because of the very real danger of a hold-up along the way. It would be very inadvisable unless driving in a convoy, just to saunter off on one of the beautiful but lawless rural back roads of Laos, however appealing the idea might seem.

There are a number of garages selling cars in Vientiane – the most common makes, predictably enough, being Japanese or French. When you buy a car make sure the company can offer a guarantee and that backup service is available too. If you buy a second hand vehicle from a foreigner, make sure that the duty has been paid on it. Some foreigners are allowed to buy a car locally or import one duty free.

You must remember to carry your road tax papers, identity card, driver's license and vehicle registration papers when driving. You must also display a sticker to show that the vehicle has passed its obligatory six month road test. You will need to have a minimum third party insurance policy for your car, though extra cover is recommended. If you intend to drive your vehicle into Thailand, you will need a temporary insurance cover. You can obtain this when you reach the exit on the Thai side of the Mittaphab Bridge.

For convenience sake some expatriates employ a Lao driver. This has the added advantage that, in the event of a serious accident, the driver, not passenger, will bear the legal responsibility. If you do have any kind of accident, keep your head and have someone call the police and your insurance company while you remain at the scene. They will decide on liability and compensation.

Petrol is quite easy to find. There seems to be plenty of private stations operating in even quite remote places. There are no limits on the amount you can buy. Don't expect to find things like unleaded petrol though. Car restraint seats for children are not available in Laos so you will have to bring your own.

HAVING PETS

Many people consider that there are enough stray animals, rodents, insects and reptiles in the Lao world as it is without voluntarily introducing more into this crowded menagerie. If you do decide you must have a pet though, your first priority will be to establish that it is healthy and can stay so. Without appearing unkind, be very circumspect about bringing animals into your home. You may end up incurring more anguish for everybody, especially children, if you have to take it along to the vet a few days later to be put down.

If you bring your own pet from home expect a lengthy quarantine period before the animal is released. This may be only the beginning of your troubles. If you bring a pet from home it may have even more problems adapting to a new environment than you do. However many vaccinations you put them through their resistance to diseases they have not been exposed to before will be low. Your dogs luxuriant, well tended fur will be a first rate home for local populations of parasites, fleas, ringworm, ticks and lord knows what. A pet bred locally will be better adjusted to the climate than a foreign one, but you should note that dogs and monkeys are the main carriers of rabies in Laos. Make sure if you do have pets that they are vaccinated regularly against common problems like rabies, hepatitis, parvovirus and distemper. If you intend to bring in vaccines from abroad, make sure they are refrigerated.

The Lao are perfectly comfortable coexisting with animals – the Buddhist concept of reincarnation precludes cruelty towards animals – but they rarely make a big fuss about their pets in the same way that Westerners or some affluent Asians do. Staff can be entrusted with looking after pets but don't expect them to be spoilt or for them to go out of their way to accommodate them.

If you intend to travel think long and hard about what the options are for your pet. If you have Lao staff on hand, there should be no problems but you may find very few of your foreign or Lao friends eager to look after a bouncy dog, malodorous rabbit or inquisitive cat. Don't expect to find dog homes or kennels in Laos. Think ahead when considering buying a pet. When the time comes to leave, an undemanding and impeccably manicured cat will be easier to find a home for than a shaggy, romping mog.

Note the conservation status of more exotic animals before you allow some hunter or dealer in rare species to persuade you to buy a krait or red leaf monkey off him. Groups like the Worldwide Fund for Nature are fighting an uphill battle in trying to set up legislation for creatures marked for the lucrative export trade in endangered species or local animals, reptiles and birds destined for the cooking pot. One Japanese couple resident in Laos appeared genuinely surprised when told by a customs official that they would not be taking their collection of hawks, red leaf monkeys and green pigeons back with them to Osaka!

Chapter Five

TOWERS OF BABEL

Lao, like most languages, is best learnt on the spot. Restricted resources and materials for learning the language will, in any case, effectively limit the amount of Lao you can learn before you arrive. Total immersion, or at least a gingerly testing of the waters of the unfamiliar sounds and symbols of Lao from as early on in your stay as possible is recommended. The more you drag your feet the harder it will be to get started.

STARTING OUT WITH LAO

Language is a great ice breaker. Even a cursory knowledge of Lao will add to your understanding of the culture, and earn you the approbation of the Lao who will be flattered and impressed that a foreigner has gone to the trouble to learn the rudiments of their language. It will make you new friends and help the Lao to take you more seriously as someone who is putting in time in their country, not just passing through. Of course, that doesn't mean that the fishmonger in the local wet market or your gardener's wife won't split their sides with laughter at your linguistic faux pas, find your accent hilarious or roll their eyes in mock horror at the way you butcher their subtle tonal system. There is rarely anything malevolent in this kind of good natured ridicule though, and if you are quick on the uptake it will give you a chance to introduce some comic banter of your own just to get even!

Standard Lao – *phaa saa laao* – as spoken by the people of Vientiane, is the official language of the LDPR and is spoken nationwide by some three million people. It is increasingly known and used among other ethnic groups in Laos, though many of these minorities still prefer to use their own dialects, switching to standard Lao when they bring their produce to market or encounter officials, social workers and the like from the towns. Laos in fact, is a Solomon's Mine for the linguist or budding anthropologist. Russian language experts sent here in the 1980s are said to have recorded over 600 distinct languages and dialects in current use in Laos. Even among speakers of standard Lao there are considerable differences in regional dialects. The people of Vientiane quip that they speak Lao, northerners sing it, and southerners bark it! Some time will elapse before you can differentiate between a talking, singing or barking Lao though.

Lao belongs to the Thai group of languages. It bears a strong resemblance to languages spoken in parts of Yunnan Province in south China, by the Shan people of northern Myanmar and among ethnic groups like the Black Thai and Ly of northern Vietnam. Its strongest link however, is with Thai which most Lao can readily understand. This particularly applies in the case of the Thai spoken in the northeast of Thailand where 17 million native Laotians, or Thai-Issan – over three times the population of Laos – speak dialects which are closer to Vientiane than Bangkok.

Older Lao in fact, can frequently be heard bewailing the influence of standard Thai, which appears to be swamping Vientiane through television and radio programs, pop music and the import of Thai magazines and papers. Many text books used in colleges and at university are in Thai. When several rooms at the Bibliotech Nationale were unlocked a couple of years ago, many scientific and technical texts in French and English were, for want of existing words in Lao, given Thai classifications and titles. Since 1975, standard Lao has gained more prominence but the government's efforts to promote it are hampered by limited printing facilities and finances.

ENCOURAGING DATA

Many opportunities to practise the language exist. Shopkeepers, samlor drivers, Lao co-workers, waiters and many other people will be only too happy to engage you in conversation or a simple exchange of pleasantries. Courtesy and an ability to listen being a prerequisite of the well bred Lao, nobody will object if you blunder on in pidgin abbreviations that would test the patience of most other races.

The script may seem inscrutable, the sounds baffling, but Lao is generally regarded as one of the easier Asian languages to learn. Syllabic languages tend generally, to be easier to learn anyway but add to this the fact that for most practical situations Lao is usually spoken in the present tense, the prospects of learning it become far less remote. Lao, like Spanish, is also a phonetic language, meaning that words are spelt the way they are pronounced unlike English or French for example, which are irregular. Naturally, you will have to be able to read the letters of the Lao alphabet before you can do this.

MASTERING THE TONAL SYSTEM

The major stumbling block for most people, unfamiliar with the way languages like Lao are modulated, is the tonal system. Although words of foreign extraction like Pali, Sanskrit and French, may have several clearly individualised syllables Lao, being essentially mono-syllabic, differentiates many of its identical phonemes exclusively by

91

Some examples of the Lao script as used to teach children.

tone. In plain language, many words carrying different meanings have exactly the same sound. The only thing that differentiates them from each other is tone. In other words, if you don't get the tone right you'll sound as if you are referring to an entirely different word. *Gai*, for instance, can mean 'fair' in the low tone, but 'near' in the high rising tone. Likewise, 'friends' in the mid tone, uttered in a low rising tone, denotes 'pigs.' You shouldn't get too fraught over tones however. A lot of people get by perfectly well as the verbal context will, in most cases, indicate quite clearly the meaning of the vocabulary you are using and what you are alluding to. Most languages are intonated to some degree anyway and as we all have different voice pitches, tones will vary from speaker to speaker. If you can resist overlaying your own intonations onto Lao you will be well on the road to making yourself understood. Here, just for the record , are definitions for the six commonly used tones in Lao.

- The low tone – Pitched at the lower range of your normal conversational voice. Even and flat.
- The mid tone – Almost the same as the above but in a fractionally higher pitch.
- The high tone – Even, pitched towards the top of your vocal range, with a slight rise near the end.
- The low rising tone – Starts a little below your normal range, softening in intensity while building up to a point equal or slightly above the high tone.
- The high rising tone – Starts in the high tone and falls quickly to the mid tone.
- The low falling tone – A quick drop in tone and intensity from mid to low tone.

These fine distinctions sound more difficult than they actually are but in order to duplicate them with perfect accuracy you need to have reasonably good listening acuity.

THE WRITTEN SCRIPT

Lao writing is based on an ancient Brahmanic script which has been modified over the centuries but retains traces of its original configurations. The slightly antiquated appearance of Lao is however, a little deceptive as the script only came into being during the Lane Xang period, but because it is based on an older script and has not been subject to the same revisions that the Thai alphabet underwent, it appears to be much older. The oldest existing documents in Lao date from the 16th century and are written on perishable palm leaf in Tham, a forerunner of *tuua laao*, a modern form of literary Lao. Like English, Lao is written from left to right.

For residents who are keen to start reading Lao there isn't really a great deal of printed matter available. Lao newspapers and a few modern novels which occasionally get printed up will be heavy going in the beginning. There are several language primers and other learning aids in the bibliography at the back of this book. A good way to get started with Lao is to visit the children's section of the Bibliotech Nationale in Vientiane which has an excellent selection of first-step readers. There are various NGOs in town helping to promote literacy and a love of books that might let you dip into their well stocked children's and young adult libraries.

Trying to transliterate the sounds of Lao can be a confusing business. It is virtually impossible to precisely render a Lao sound if, for example, it doesn't exist in English. Even among speakers of the same language there will be considerable differences in the interpretation of one sound. Even a simple enough sound can be phoneticised in many ways – 'bao,' 'ban,' 'bo,' 'baw,' and 'boor' and so on. It doesn't really matter if you are just jotting down Lao words as you hear them for your own purposes, but if you are using a text or primer of some sort you will have to check off the phonetic system being used against the sounds as you hear them and stick to that method for as long as you are following their material. Many of the transcriptions that we have are French approximations of Lao sounds which are of more limited use to English speakers.

Consonants and Vowels

There are 33 consonants in Lao, falling into three different groups according to low, high and rising tones. But because almost all the consonants in the high and rising category share the same sound this reduces the actual number of different sounds to only 20, all of which exist, more or less, in English. Some of them, like 'bp' or 'ng,' look odd at the beginning of a word as we are more accustomed to seeing them combined in the middle or at the end of a sentence. Two letters, commonly transcribed as 'v' and 'x' are the source of endless confusion. 'V' is closer to an English 'w' and the 'x' like our 's' or 'z.' The small northern town of Vieng Xai for example, is more likely to sound like 'Wieng Sai'. Likewise, you will hear the district of Xieng Khouang coming out more like 'Zien Ngoen.' You'll soon get used to cases like these.

The Lao language has 28 vowel sounds, most of which are pronounced as they are in English. These can be divided into two types: long and short. These sounds themselves differ from each other only in length, not sound. For example:

- a short 'u' – *puk* (to wake up)
- a long 'u' – *puuak* (termites)

Most primers transcribe the longer vowel sound with double letters to avoid misunderstandings. Most diphthongs and tripthongs, like 'ia' and 'yai,' are pronounced as one sound. Again, be aware of French transliterations and place names in particular, many of which are still extant.

BUILDING BLOCKS

Lao sentences follow a subject-verb-object pattern, so that the word order of a phrase like "The sampan brought lotus flowers over the river" would be much the same in Lao as in English. To make verbs or adjectives negative, the word *baw* is placed before the word, as in

95

koy who-tchac lao (I know him), and *kow baw who-tchak lao* (I don't know him). You can also add *baw* to the end of a sentence to form a rhetorical question or to elicit an affirmative response, such as "The festival is next week, isn't it?"

Question words like 'what,' 'how' and 'which' usually fall at the end of a sentence. 'How much,' for example, is *tao dai*, so in a sentence like "How much does it come to?" you would say *la ka tao dai*. When asking questions in Lao you shouldn't raise your voice at the end of a question as we do in English. If there is any emphasis at all in Lao it is likely to occur when positively emphasising a verb. Adjectives follow the nouns they modify as in Latin languages. 'Ripe' is *suk-du* a 'ripe papaya' will be *maak-hung suk-du*.

Gender, tense and number are consistent in Lao, with the exception of pronouns where *phuak* is generally added to make *phuak lao* (they) rather than 'he' or 'she,' which is just *lao*. Tenses are not conjugated as they are in many languages but indicated by qualifiers like *laew* for the past and *tja* and *si* placed before the verb to demonstrate future. It is quite common to use words like 'tomorrow,' 'yesterday' and 'in four days' to indicate time, rather than verb qualifiers.

FRANCAISE OU ANGLAISE?

Probably the latter these days, given the inexorable rise of English as the preferred second language for most Southeast Asian countries. French, as in other parts of Indo-China, has entered into terminal decline. Many educated Lao over the age of 50 however, speak the language very well. There are still traces of French to be found in shop signs, restaurant menus and designations like Electricite du Laos. French tourists form the largest contingent of non-Asian visitors to the country so there continues to be a need for qualified French speakers.

Officially, French remains the second language at government level and legal documents written in French are still sometimes presented to foreigners. It is highly unlikely that French will ever regain its former standing in Laos. The same goes for Russian. "Three years in Leningrad," a Lao friend, sent abroad to attend a language program and now hastily learning English, laments, "and suddenly all the Soviet people are recalled from Laos!" English will, without question, establish itself as the main lingua franca of international communication in Laos.

NAMES, GREETINGS AND PROTOCOLS

Most Lao have just two names: their given – *syy* – and family name – *naamsakun* – in that order. Family names were only adopted by the majority of Lao in 1943 so some people, especially older rural folk, do not possess one. It is not the habit to use family names much at all in Laos, though a lot of foreigners, hard pressed to remember which Boun, Bouchanh or Bounmy is which, would no doubt like to see a wider use made of surnames!

Given names are used for most purposes, family names mostly for official purposes. Family names are almost never used alone. People often go for years without knowing a co-worker or neighbour's surname. Family and close friends usually use nicknames for each other. These often take the form of diminutives like *La* for Khamla. It is quite common for someone who believes that their current name is attracting bad luck or ill health, to change it.

Depending upon age, social standing, sex, profession and so on, different forms of address are used. The use of the correct term of address is quite important, establishing as it does the relative degree of respect and politeness due. The honorific prefix *nay* for instance, is used when addressing relatives of parental or older age. If you wish to convey to a non-relative that you hold him or her in equal respect to your own relatives, you can employ honorific prefixes like *poh* (father), *mae* (mother) and *ay* (older brother).

Different forms of address will be used for monks, doctors, younger people, equals and many others. You should try and learn as many of the appropriate categories as you can. It's also worth noting that selecting the correct pronoun when referring to yourself is important if you wish to avoid causing offence or dismay. When referring to yourself you should choose a pronoun relative to how you perceive your own standing to that person. This can range from the faintly Victorian 'Your servant' – *khaa-phatjao* – 'literally slave your' to the intimate *hao*. When talking about yourself in the company of close friends for example, you could use the pronoun *koo*. *Khao* would be used to indicate 'I' with strangers deemed to be the same age or older than you; *khanoi* when addressing a person or someone highly esteemed in Lao society, such as a teacher; and *han* as a generic, neutral term but one which should never be used towards someone to whom respect is due. Most Lao feel comfortable addressing foreigners with polite prefixes like Mr. or Miss., which are often combined with our given names, as in Mr. John or Miss Anne. This is often done even when they know it is not generally the custom among foreigners to do so.

There is no exact equivalent to 'good morning/afternoon/evening' in Lao. The most useful greeting is *sabadee* an all-purpose 'good day' to which the response is the same. More colloquial greetings you may hear used among friends or people of roughly the same age or a little younger, include *chang dia* – 'How are things?' or *pai sai* – literally 'Where are you going?' The same greetings can be used, with the addition of the respectful *khanoi*, when addressing older people or superiors.

PARTING WORDS

Traditionally, the *nop* (*wai* in Thailand), a gracious, prayer-like gesture in which both hands are lightly clasped together at chest height, with a simple *lah-gohn* (goodbye), is the usual kind of leave taking. Young or urban Lao are just as likely to shake hands these days. The most common reply to the above is *sook dii* (good luck). *Phop kan mai* (See you later) is another popular form. The response in this case is the same but respect can be transmitted by combining it with the suitable kinship term or name.

USEFUL WORDS AND PHRASES

General

- How are you?   *Chao sabadee baw?*
- Goodbye   *Lah-gohn*
- Yes/No   *men/baw*
- Thank you   *kop-chai*
- Good   *dee*
- Bad   *baw-dee* (lit. 'not good')
- I'm going to …   *koy pie …*
- What is this?   *Ahn-nee men nyung?*
- Do you have …?   *Chao me … baw?*
- I don't understand   *Koy baw co-chi*
- I don't know   *Koy baw who-tchak*
- What is your name?   *Jao maa tae sai?*

Shopping And Food

- market   *thalat*
- How much is this?   *Ahn-neetaw die?*
- food   *ah-han*
- rice   *kao*
- expensive/cheap   *pheng/touk*
- restaurant   *lahn ah-han*
- tea/hot tea   *nam sa/nam sa hawn*
- coffee   *kah-fay*
- noodle soup   *me nam*
- delicious   *sehb*
- I would like to eat …   *Koy yahk kin …*
- fruit   *maak-mai*
- chicken   *kai*
- fish   *paa*
- vegetable   *phak*

Numbers

1	*nung*	11	*sip-et*
2	*song*	12	*sip-song*
3	*sahm*	13	*sip-sahn*
4	*see*	20	*sao*
5	*hah*	21	*sao-et*
6	*hoke*	30	*sahn-sip*
7	*chet*	35	*sahn-hah*
8	*pet*	100	*hoy-nung*
9	*cow*	200	*song hoy*
10	*sip*	1000	*pahn*

Days and Dates

- Monday   *Van-tyan*
- Tuesday   *Van-angkhaan*
- Wednesday   *Van-phut*
- Thursday   *Van-phatat*
- Friday   *Van-suk*
- Saturday   *Van-sao*
- Sunday   *Van-aathit*
- Today   *myy nii*
- Tomorrow   *myy yyn*
- Yesterday   *myy-vaan-nil*
- This week   *aathit nii*
- This month   *dyyan nii*
- This year   *pii nil*
- Some time   *myy naa*
- Now   *veelaa nii*
- Morning   *muh-sao*
- Afternoon   *thon-sao*
- Evening   *muh-leng*
- Night   *muh-kuhn*

Around Town

- pedicab   *sahm-law*
- taxi loht   *doy-sahn*
- bus   *loht buht*
- aeroplane   *hena bin*
- policeman   *tham-louaht*
- shop   *haan-khaa*
- school   *hong-hien*
- embassy   *sathaanthuut*
- cafe   *kin deum*
- office   *hawng kaan*
- post office   *pai-sa-nii*

Emergencies

- I am sick   *Khawy pen jep*
- doctor   *maw*
- hospital   *'honng pha-yaa-baan*
- How do I get to … ? *pai thaang dai … ?*

Lao novice monks taking a break to read some imported Thai comics.

SCHOOLS, COURSES AND TUTORS

There are several language schools in Vientiane that run regular courses for foreigners. These range form beginner to advanced classes, both group and private tuition. Some of the best known are the Lao-American Language Centre, the Mittaphab School, the Saysettha Language Centre and the Advanced Training Centre (ATC) which also offers courses in Lao culture. The Centre de Langue Francaise de Vientiane also runs courses in Lao. If you have always meant to learn French but never had the time, there are many opportunities to study the French language and culture in Vientiane.

Advertisements for group or private lessons in Lao are sometimes displayed on the notice boards of expatriate clubs, international schools, or in the windows of mini-marts. Information on courses also appears occasionally in the *Vientiane Times* and *Discover Laos*, a monthly travel magazine. You may also be able to make contact through work or social circles with Lao people prepared to agree to Lao-English language exchange sessions. There are many urban Lao now interested in learning English but without the financial means to engage a private tutor or join a language school.

Chapter Six

PEOPLE

The Cambodians plant the rice,
The Vietnamese harvest the rice,
The Laotians listen to the rice grow.

—Indo-Chinese Proverb

The Lao population though low, consists of an extraordinary variety of ethnic groups whose diversity and, in some cases isolation, has made the realisation of true cultural and political unity in Laos difficult. Historically, the country has always been ruled by the dominant Lao, or Lao Lum, and their leadership has often reflected, at least until recent times, the ideas and aspirations of the Lao elite rather than the attitudes and activities of the minorities.

The Lao Lum account for roughly 55% of the population. The government claims that the number of ethnic groups in Laos totals 68, but if you include the various branches and subgroups of these tribes as well as outsiders like the Vietnamese, ethnic Chinese, Indians and Thais who are found in many large towns, the range and diversity found in this tiny population is truly staggering, and a source of inexhaustible interest for ethnologists, visitors and residents alike.

The Lao Lum occupy the Mekong plains and the alluvial strands of land along its tributaries, while the tribal peoples tend on the whole, to live at higher altitudes in relatively small groups. It is this vertical pattern of ethnic distribution which has an important bearing on the country's political and geographic unity. More as a strategy to promote a sense of national unity than accuracy, the country's ethnic groups have been categorised into three broad bands based on the relationship between altitude and habitat: lum, theung and soung, signifying valley, slope and high place, define both the ethnography and homelands of these groups.

AN ELEVATED PEOPLE

The Lao Lum are a subgroup of the Tai peoples believed to have occupied most of what is now Yunnan province in southwest China. Sedentary wet-rice cultivators and Theravada Buddhists, the Lao Lum together with other Tai neighbours, underwent a long period of acculturation to Indian ideas. Unlike the Cambodians to the southwest who speak languages derived from a Mon-Khmer stock, the Lao along with their neighbours in Thailand, speak Tai languages of Sino-Tibetan origin.

Adept in the techniques of wet-rice agriculture as well as the military arts, both learnt from the Chinese, the Lao quickly gained mastery of the Mekong flood plains, a position that enabled them to become the undisputed architects of the nation's chief institutions and traditions. The Lao spoken by the lowlanders remains the official language of Laos and Theravada Buddhism, strongly associated with the Lao Lum, its main religion.

TAI GROUPS

The Lao Tai share the same origins as the Lao Lum and their languages are mutually intelligible. The Tai tribes mostly inhabit the mountain valleys of northern Laos, subsisting as wet-rice growers as well as cultivating such staples as millet, corn, sweet potatoes and

A Lao Lum hunter encountered on the road.

beans. Mountain slopes are used for wheat and dry rice. The Lao Tai differ most from the Lao Lum in their spirit beliefs and practices which are largely animistic, with vague Buddhist, Confucianist and Taoist accretions. The Lao Tai are great believers in *phi*, or spirits, and will go to great lengths to appease the more malevolent or mischievous variety of genii. Tai society is organised into confederacies of tribes called *muongs*, meaning districts. Each muong is presided over by an elected council of chieftains or headmen.

LAO THEUNG

Of Austro-Indonesian extraction, the Lao Theung, the country's midland dwellers, form the largest minority group in Laos. The Lao Theung normally inhabit altitudes above river valleys but generally below the 1000 metre mark reserved for higher dwellers. The languages and dialects of the Lao Theung belong to the Mon-Khmer language family. No writing systems exist. Lao Theung groups like the Khmu are scattered all over the country but the largest concentrations can be found in the north and on the fertile Bolovens Plateau in southern Laos. Favoured crops include rice, maize, cotton, tobacco and legumes. Traditionally, the Lao Theung are semi-nomadic in their agricultural habits and considerable problems have arisen from their practice of slash-and-burn, or swidden cultivation in which large tracts of hillside are fired and then abandoned once exhausted. They also hunt and gather an increasingly depleted stock of animals and forest products as well as raising livestock such as chickens, pigs and occasionally cattle. One of the most important events in the Lao Theung calendar is the annual sacrifice of buffaloes. Their position in Lao society has always been rather lower than other ethnic groups, and this is reflected in their relatively low standards of living. The Lao Theung, referred to until quite recently by the pejorative term *kha* (slave), are accustomed to hire themselves out as day labourers to more prosperous Lao farmers or even to cross into Thailand to offer their services in return for the hard currency that will enable them to buy buffaloes, manufactured cloth and the metal gongs and drums which continue to be highly prized and constitute part of a village's assets. Some Lao Theung groups have become assimilated into mainstream Lao culture, even adopting its language as their own, but the majority remain doggedly independent and will often, save for the practical realities of the market place, have little or nothing to do with their lowland neighbours.

LAO SOUNG

The Lao Soung, the nation's highlanders, are the most recent settlers in Laos, many having migrated from China only in the past 200 years. Important Lao Soung groups include the Hmong, Akha and Man (or Yao). Their languages are related to the Chinese, or Tibeto-Burman family and their features, which are discernibly more Mongolian than other Lao, speak instantly of their provenance. Other Lao in fact, refer to them as the Chinese Group. Their spirit practices, which are essentially animist, are also partly influenced by Chinese Buddhism and Confucianism.

The Lao Soung further disassociate themselves from other groups by their choice of physical location, showing a preference for altitudes above 1000 metres. Large concentrations of Lao Soung are found in the north, northwest and especially in the province of Xieng Khouane. The Lao Soung are also swidden farmers, raising rice and corn as their main staples, but are also, and more notoriously known for their cultivation of opium, a cash crop that has helped them to remain economically self-sufficient.

Fiercely independent and opting to live in the most elevated and therefore, most inaccessible regions of the country, the Lao Soung have been the least willing to surrender their hard earned cultural autonomy. The Lao Soung regard themselves as free to cross the borders of adjacent countries at will and their communities can be found in the highlands of Thailand, southern China and Myanmar as well as Laos.

A Yao elder in the remote northwest of the country.

Well disciplined and with a long martial tradition, many Hmong groups were inducted into the royal army during the civil war or were on the payroll of the CIA during the Vietnam War when America conducted secret operations within Laos. More than 10,000 Hmong died in action during the 1960s and countless more fled the country after the Communist takeover. Although referred to derogatively by both the French and Lao as *Meo*, a Chinese word meaning 'barbarian,' the Hmong have succeeded in overcoming much of the prejudice historically directed towards them and have, because of their tough, uncompromising character, earned the grudging respect of many other Lao groups.

Unlike lowlanders, the Hmong build their houses firmly on the ground, not on stilts. Extended families live within the same house, each family belonging to a clan led by its eldest male. It is the responsibility of the clan leader to communicate with the family's ancestors and with the spirit world in general. A village headman, generally the clan leader of the wealthiest family in the community, is elected by the village. The village headman wields considerable power, not only as administrator of tribal affairs but also as judge and arbitrator in legal disputes.

Akha

Pass under a wooden gate like a raised door jam with two wooden male and female figures placed just inside, and you know that you have entered an Akha village. The Akha, who share the same southern Chinese roots common to many Lao tribes, are also shifting cultivators who place a high importance on what they collectively refer to as the 'Akha Way,' a complicated system of belief which involves among other things, the memorising and reciting of their oral myths and the names of all their male ancestors, a formidable task. The Akha, are instantly recognisable from the clothing of their women who are fond of sporting a colourful line in headdresses adorned with beads and old silver colonial coins, appliqued homespun cloth, short skirts and tight leggings. The distinctive ceremonies and rituals of the Akha and their desire to remain as elusive as possible, have always set them apart from other Lao groups. The difficulties the Akha face in reconciling their culture with the encroaching world and the increasing difficulties they have underwriting their costly and time consuming rituals, have put considerable pressure on this group. Opium addiction among the Akha is depressingly high.

Smoking a mild, home-grown tobacco among tribes like the Alak and Laven of southern Laos, begins as early as three or four years of age.

Man

The Man, also known as the Yao and Mien are, like the Akha, a reclusive people preoccupied with making ritual offerings to the spirits as a means of earning merit and higher ranking in the after life. The Man also practice a highly ritualistic form of Taoism that was common in the China of the 13th and 14th centuries. The largest number of Man communities are found in and around the province of Nam Tha, in the heart of the Lao section of the Golden Triangle. The Man are accomplished craftsmen, producing complex silver jewellery, crossbows, rifles and well tempered knives. They are unusual among Lao hill tribes for possessing a sophisticated writing script based on Chinese ideograms. Man houses, always built on the ground, and with a carefully positioned ancestral altar, accommodate large extended families and can be quite crowded. The Man women, with their black and red turbans and indigo slacks and the children with embroidered skull caps and red pom poms immediately announce their tribal affiliation. The Man in fact, have been described as "the most elegantly dressed but worst housed people in the world."

The Man, who have no combative traditions to speak of, have a reputation for being peace makers and will go to great lengths to reconcile differences or to mend fences between disputing parties.

HILL TRIBE ETIQUETTE

You are almost certain while you are living in Laos to want, sooner or later, to see how the 'other half' lives. Whether visiting an ethnic minority village near a large town or way out in the remoter regions, there are certain general guidelines that should be followed in order not to cause offence. If you stick to them you might even be invited back to a village to witness one of its important festivals or ceremonies, a great honour and an experience that you are unlikely to forget.

Visitors should try to find out as much as they can before setting off on a trip to visit an ethnic village as etiquette and customs vary considerably between one tribe and another. In the case of the Akha

A young member of the Ippo tribe has been alloted the task of chopping wood.

for example, it would be a serious blunder to defile one of their sacred gates by touching one of its posts or by entering under its arches if you didn't intend going into one of the houses in the village. You will probably be accompanied by a Lao person in the form of a guide or acquaintance of the village so you should ask as many questions as possible to avoid making mistakes of this sort.

Entrances of one sort or another often carry a lot of symbolism so check first before stepping or sitting, for example, on someone's door step or passing under a door lintel. Although many tribal people may be perfectly happy to be photographed – you should always send or deliver prints to them later – there are many taboos against photographing sacred images, spirit groves, shrines and sacrificial areas that you should first gain clearance for. Always dress modestly and never change or undress in front of people. Ostentatious displays of wealth are an obvious insensitivity. So too are inappropriate gifts. Food is always readily accepted but again, take some time to think of the circumstances in which the recipients live. A bag of dried chillies or some packets of vegetable or herb seeds will be far more appreciated in the long run than a copy watch or Christmas pudding!

— *Chapter Seven* —

RELIGION: A WAY OF LIFE

Laotians hold in high esteem any freaks of nature, especially when they take the form of a cavern which may be utilised as a place of worship.

—19th century traveller to Laos

The Lao way of life, strongly influenced as it is by a combination of spirit worship, animism and the country's distinctive school of Theravada, or Hinayanist Buddhism, is something the average Lao rarely gives much conscious thought to and which he characteristically refrains from forcing on others. Few of us are ever fully aware of the degree to which our own cultures shape and prescribe our daily lives, but as foreigners in a foreign land many expatriates find that they are more alert than they normally would be to the relationship between belief and such things as the perception of time, death, the moral code, social intercourse and traditional solutions to the problems of life.

Lao Buddhism, the dominant faith of the majority of the population, is said to be highly syncretic, overlaid as it is with a belief in *phi* (animist spirits), a cult that predates Buddhism in Laos. Phi are believed to exercise great power over the destinies of men and the cult is found in some form everywhere in Laos today, even quite often, among the ranks of the Buddhist clergy. The absorption of elements of phi worship into formal Buddhist practices over hundreds of years has created a situation many foreigners initially find hard to grasp, in which *bonzes* (monks) are often seen participating side by side with a village sorcerer or shaman in the propitiation or exorcising of phi.

Every Lao Lum town has at least one *wat*, which is often the most conspicuous building in sight. Wats usually consist of a temple or sim, a large wooden or brick meeting hall and bungalows or dormitories housing members of the monastery. At various times in the Buddhist calendar, impromptu stages are erected for the holding of ceremonies, festivals and fairs which hold considerable importance for the religious, social and economic life of the community. After a few visits to your local wat it will soon become apparent that they service not only the spiritual needs of the community but also provide much of its entertainment and diversion. Despite attempts by the revolutionary government to reduce its influence, Buddhism continues to be one of the main social forces in Laos. A softening in the government's policies towards Buddhism in the 1980s spurred a revival of the faith, a fact evident in the number of redecorated and restored wats, the practice of alms giving, and increased attendance figures at religious festivals, many of which were formerly banned.

Whether as followers of Buddhism, animism, primitive Brahmanism, ancestor worship, diluted forms of Confucianism or the deeply ingrained practice of spirit appeasement, almost all Lao expend a great deal of effort on the gaining of merit. In this way a large portion of a family's savings are directed towards the attainment of essentially nonmaterial goals. Traditionally, the Lao have always disapproved of the accumulation of personal wealth. Poverty and penury, with their strong identification with spirituality, have always been more respected. Like everything else in the developing world, this ideal sits rather uncomfortably alongside new, more materialistic values.

BUDDHISM

Theravada, or Hinayana Buddhism as it is sometimes called, is the official religion of Laos. Closer to the original more stringent teachings of the Buddha himself and a more demanding school than the widely practised doctrine of Mahayana Buddhism, Theravada Buddhism, offers a direct path to nirvana to only a few ascetics.

Although archeologists have unearthed remains of carved Buddhas dating from the 12th century, the earliest historical record of Buddhism in Laos dates from 1356 with the arrival of the Phra Bang, a Singhalese carving presented to the Lao king, Fa Ngum, by a Khmer mission of Theravada Buddhists.

The essence of Buddhism is contained in the Four Noble Truths which can be summed up in the Buddha's conclusion that all life entails suffering and that the cause of suffering is desire. Only the extinction of cravings by detachment from all things, including the self, can break the cycle of suffering and help us attain Nirvana, a word that can be roughly translated as 'extinction of the self.' Buddhism is highly causative. The concept of karma holds that man is responsible for his actions in both his present and former lives and that evil actions must be atoned for by suffering in present and future lives. Suffering as a result of past actions is unavoidable but meritorious acts in this life can improve our lot in the next.

The way to achieve this is by following the Eight Fold Path. Simply stated, this requires: right understanding, right purpose, right speech, right conduct, right vocation, right effort, right thinking and right meditation. A person's karma can also be improved and a better condition in the next life attained by following Buddhism's basic rules of moral conduct, which include prohibitions on killing any living thing, falsehood, stealing, incontinence, and the drinking of alcohol.

It is still the custom, whenever possible, for young men to become novice monks, although the period of service is likely to be much shorter these days than before.

These rules, which are more in the nature of guidelines, have never been rigorously enforced, and such things as religious or sectarian wars or inquisitions inspired by Buddhism are unknown. One of the much remarked upon characteristics of Buddhism in fact, is its remarkable tolerance and its touching acceptance of man's fallibility. Neither authoritarian, prescriptive or exclusive in its attitude towards its followers or other religions, Buddhism simply offers a way forward for those who wish to follow it.

Merit and Monks

In normal, everyday life there are a number of ways in which merit can be gained. These include offering food and alms to monks, supporting your local temple with monetary gifts, becoming a monk for a period of time or dedicating a son into the monkhood. It is often women in Laos, especially older women, who present food to monks. Other offerings include flowers, fruit, incense and gold leaf which is pressed onto images of the Buddha. Traditionally, young men are expected to spend a period of three months living and studying in a monastery. This practice still has significance in Laos, though it appears to be less widespread than before. Those who do become bonzes, if only for a short time, are held in high esteem by Lao society, and great honour is conferred on the family. One popular belief among the optimistic Lao is that a family whose son has entered the monkhood will be spared the torments of hell.

Monks are not productive in the material sense since their vows prohibit them from working but they are involved in a number of ways in the life of the community and perform a number of important functions. They officiate at all formal religious festivals and lay ceremonies such as the dedication of a new house or opening of a new business. Their presence is indispensable at marriages, funerals and the naming ceremonies of infants.

A Few House Rules

When visiting a Lao wat or coming into contact with monks or religious materials, there are a few things you should bear in mind. It goes without saying that decent clothing is a must for entering any temple or compound. If you enter a religious building, particularly a *sim*, the central chapel, always take off your shoes. And don't carry them around with you as some people do. They will be perfectly safe outside. Unless they are stuffed with cash and credit cards like a Christmas stocking, nobody would think of pinching them!

If you happen to be carrying a book or magazine on Buddhism, a guide to temples or holy sites or other publications of this sort, try to treat them with a touch more reverence than you would a novel or newspaper. It would pain a Lao to see a beer stain forming across the image of a respected abbot or a sun hat thrown over the cover of a book on Buddhist art.

It is usually acceptable to photograph Buddha images but posing in front of sacred objects or, worse still, clambering over them to pose for a picture is definitely out. If you would like to sit in front of a Buddha image, make sure that your feet are tucked beneath you or otherwise pointed away from it.

119

Women should never touch a monk or his robe. If they wish to give something to a monk this should be made clear to him. He will then extend a part of his robe to receive the offering. Otherwise objects can be placed on a clean surface such as a table or shelf. In temples you will see that monks often sit on platforms. This is because no one should sit with their head higher than a monk. These gestures of obeisance are sometimes a little awkward to manage in practice without looking contrived, particularly for lanky foreigners standing facing a monk. Modest entrance fees are charged for some of the more important religious sites in the capital but where these do not exist a small donation placed in the offertory box or on the floor near the central image will be much appreciated.

Restrictions of this sort may seem excessive, especially when it is quite common in Laos to see slightly louche young monks strolling across temple compounds or in the vicinity of sacred images puffing on cigarettes, but that is the way it is!

A Buddhist–Animist Melange

Though Buddhism doesn't recognise the existence of an independent soul in the Western religious sense the Lao, in common with the Thai, believe in the idea of a 'mobile soul,' or spirit, which the Lao call the *khouan*. When resident in the body (generally the head) it is the source of well-being. Should the *khouan* wander, be startled out of the body or forced out by a malign phi, the body will sicken and, in some cases, die. Phi are believed to inhabit all animate and inanimate forms of nature such as rocks, trees, streams, fire and so on, as well as Lao houses. Most Lao households contain two altars: one to the Lord Buddha and another, no less important, dedicated to the phi.

An ancient and pervasive animism in which spirits exercise great power and influence over the destinies of men, predates Buddhism by many centuries and exerts a hold over the average Lao which cannot be overstated. The Communist government's attempts to ban phi worship in the 1970s seem to have met with as little success as King

A novice monk coming to grips with advanced photography.

Photisarath's decree of 1527 ordering the suppression of the cult. Phi worship is found today in some form almost everywhere in Laos.

There are a bewildering number of phi and foreigners are often amazed at how the Lao keep track of them all. Once you start looking you will begin to see evidence of the spirit world everywhere. At Wat Si Muang in Vientiane, devotees make their offerings not at the feet of the temple's main Buddhist image, but before a Khmer stone called the *lak muang*, or foundation stone, in which it is believed the spirit guardian of the city resides.

The wearing of protective tattoos is still quite common, especially in remote villages, and amulets worn for the same purpose, are sold in many temple compounds. Astrologers and other kinds of divinators are often consulted, and even in urban areas it is quite common to come across spirit mediums whose ability to make contact with the spirit world and occasionally relay messages from the dead and departed, is much in demand. The clientele of one busy medium I

121

knew included, beside the usual local villagers, a number of Buddhist monks and a minister in the government. A good deal of effort is expended by the Lao in keeping on good terms with the spirit world. Evil phi, such as the notorious *phi phetu*, are prevented from combining with other spirits for rebirth in a new body. Malevolent phi may also cause diseases many Lao believe. These must be exorcised by shamans with special knowledge of phi. Don't be jinxed by all the talk you hear about the supernatural though. Coexisting with the phi is a part of everyday life in Laos. It may seem extraordinary to outsiders but most foreigners soon accustom themselves to such things.

MINORITY CULTS

The jungles, forests and remote highlands of Laos are inhabited and guarded by an especially potent host of phi, whose existence makes these wild, relatively unknown areas fearsome places for the unwary. It is hardly surprising to find that many ethnic minorities follow their own idiosyncratic forms of spirit worship, sometimes with a mixture of Buddhism.

Among the tribal Tai for example, ancestor worship through the intermediary of phi is common. For the Black Tai the gods of the soil are the paramount deities and complex rituals connected to rice cultivation are an important part of their belief system. Among the strongly Sinicised Hmong and tribes of the north, Taoist and Confucian influences can be recognised. The Man practice a combination of animism and ancestor worship, presided over by local sorcerers and shamans.

Among some Lao Theung groups, tribes trace their ancestry back to certain animals. A belief in reincarnation is also common and each house has its own resident spirits which must be constantly and tiresomely appeased. Shamans are consulted for their powers of divination and geomancy when the time comes for a village to move to a new site.

Visitors can get a flavour of the syncretic approach to religion especially common in rural areas by attending an event like the Wat

Phu festival in February in which a buffalo is sacrificed at the site of an ancient and important Khmer-Hindu temple that was later converted to a Buddhist place of worship.

THE BACI CEREMONY

To succeed in any new enterprise or undertaking, to ensure that an already sick person's health does not deteriorate further, or to ensure the safety of those about to embark on a journey, it is necessary to have the support of the phi. As a resident you are bound, sooner or later, to be invited to take part in a *baci* (also called *sukwan*) ceremony, a uniquely Lao event that predates Lao Buddhism. Baci are performed at almost all Lao festivals and celebrations. Apart from conveying goodwill and hospitality, baci help to restore harmony and balance to both the individual and the community.

A family holding an open-air baci.

A handmade *phakhouan* tree is decked out with flowers and banana leaves and its base surrounded by symbolic food offerings. A person's 32 spirits, known as *khwan*, are tied to guests wrists by strips of white cotton. For maximum efficacy, you should leave the knots on until they fall apart of their own accord. A generous meal is served which is traditionally followed by the *lamvong*, a circle dance, although slightly abridged versions of the baci are sometimes put on. Guests at a baci are expected to join in all the stages of this graceful ritual. An invitation to a baci, with its musical accompaniment and recitations in Pali, is a window on Lao culture every foreigner should eagerly avail themselves of when the opportunity presents itself.

OTHER RELIGIONS

Foreign missionaries were expelled from Laos in 1975 but with more religious tolerance there has been a small rekindling of Christianity in Laos, although the number of converts remains low and the influence of Christianity on the social order slight. Content with their own deeply ingrained melange of Buddhism and animism, the Lao in general have been more inclined to apathy than hostility in their attitude towards those who have tried to introduce new religious beliefs. Few Buddhists have converted to Christianity but the faith has gained a toehold among some of the animist hill tribes such as the Hmong. There are said to be about 18,000 Christians in the country, but generally speaking the Lao have shown little desire to adopt the disciplines of new faiths that have no roots in their own traditions and social environment.

There are only two small mosques in the whole of Laos. The one in Vientiane holds its main services on Fridays as is the custom throughout the Islamic world. Many of its congregation, mostly of Indian extraction, are married to Lao women who have converted to Islam. The Imam here claims there are about 250 Muslim residents in Laos.

Chapter Eight

TWO WAY PERCEPTIONS: A LAOTIAN LOOKING GLASS

GOING ON ABOUT FINES FOR
BEING BAD TEMPERED ONLY
MAKES YOUR FATHER WORSE!

> The Kingdom condemns to pay a fine without any other
> formality not only those who are so carried away by their
> anger as to abuse and insult another, but also even those
> who show public contempt for others and who address
> them in too proud a manner.
>
> —Father Felippo de Marini, 17th century Jesuit

They don't fine you any more in Laos for being short tempered,
displaying contempt or untoward pride towards your fellows, but your
personal standing among the Lao will suffer just as much now as it would
have done when the above observation was made. It may sound like one
of those much peddled oriental stereotypes, and perhaps it has become
so in many more rapidly changing areas of the East, but the fact remains
that the establishing and maintenance of social harmony continues to be
a very highly valued goal in Lao society, and anything that potentially
threatens such harmony is discouraged.

In their dealings with each other, people are required to be considerate, respectful and cheerful. The Lao, in common with other nationalities, have their own way of dealing with people who overstep the social proprieties. A Lao customer in a small supermarket I happened to be in once, for example, asked for a certain commodity. The assistant duly handed it over with the change and the charming, unforced smile so characteristic of the Lao. A moment later a foreigner, clearly in a hurry, entered and, in a gruff and brusque manner ordered the same thing, only to be told by the same assistant, and in the most polite way imaginable, that they were out of stock. Being 'out of stock' in a situation like this, is a standard Lao response to bluntness or condescension.

OPINIONS, AGREEMENT AND COMPLAINTS

While overt displays of emotion, particularly anger or irritation, are clearly frowned upon, openly disagreeing with others or offering direct opinions are also discouraged as they too can be construed as disrespectful. Young people, or those of subordinate rank, are generally very loath to disagree with older people or those of superior status and will often go as far as to advance reasons supporting a superior's point of view even if they hold an entirely contrary opinion. If it becomes absolutely vital to express an opposing opinion, this is done very tentatively. It is more common for people in situations like this, especially at work, to simply remain silent. Similarly, people of so-called inferior rank or age, do not expect to be consulted as far as the decision making process goes.

Within the family or between friends, disagreements are likely to be mediated by other members of the group. This is deemed useful and necessary if one is to avoid, or at least tone down, direct confrontation. While it is normal to express one's preferences without reserve, people seldom talk at length about their likes or dislikes as this is felt to be of little interest to others. If opinions of this sort are expressed it is usually in a restrained manner. Others will usually remain silent rather than disagree.

The Lao rarely complain directly, although it is quite normal to hear people grumbling aloud to themselves when they are within earshot of the person towards whom the complaint, in a Western country, would be vociferously directed! Between friends it is more common to attribute blame to a third person. Because of the high status in which people like teachers are held, complaints often take the roundabout form of suggestions or inquiries. Rather than make a scene about, for example, substandard food or service in a restaurant, a Lao is more likely to hold his tongue, but also his patronage of the offending establishment in the future.

In general, complaints are avoided not only because they create disharmony but because it is felt that nothing can be done to alter the way things are. Complaining therefore, is just a waste of time and valuable energy. This brings us to a very important concept, and one that is dear to all Lao.

THE PRINCIPAL OF BO PEHN NGAN

Any situation a Lao believes himself powerless to do much about, or circumstances understood to be in some way preordained, regardless of how much effort is expended in trying to deflect fate, are accepted as unalterable. In the same way that we are apt to shrug our shoulders, pronounced a quick and decisive, "Oh well, it can't be helped," the Lao resort to *"Bo pehn ngan,"* which means, depending upon the situation, "Forget it," "There's nothing to be done," "Its going to be alright," and "There's no use crying over spilt milk." What distinguishes the use of this expression from similar sentiments found in other countries, among other things, is the sheer number of times you come across it. The chances are that you'll hear it at least once every day of your stay in Laos.

You shouldn't jump to the conclusion though that nothing really matters to the Lao or that they are content to simply let things take their own course, although this may often appear to be the case. Higher thresholds of tolerance and patience, together with a strong sense of predeterminism, are at the root of what many foreigners put down to lack of resolve in problem solving or a weak will. A Lao who has waited for what your average Westerner would regard as an inordinately long length of time to have a couple of electric points installed, is quite likely to shrug his shoulders and excuse the delay with a comment like "They're the experts, so they know best." Only some-one like a Lao exile perhaps, back home after a 20-year stay in the States, would be heard balling out, "So, what took you guys so long?"

Bo penh ngan may seem inadequate at times, but as a social lubricant it certainly has its uses. If you don't, to some extent, accept the way things are and allow yourself instead to become over excited, fraught or openly rude, you will be in danger of losing face.

THE CONCEPT OF FACE

Broadly speaking, there are two types of foreign residents in Laos: those who, wherever they are in the world, find cultural differences endlessly fascinating, and those who are endlessly frustrated by them. The latter definitely run more risk of losing face in front of the Lao.

To some extent of course, losing face is a universal enough idea. After all, nobody wants to look foolish in front of friends or peers, or to be held up to public ridicule, but the manner in which one loses face in Laos, and among many other Eastern races, is somewhat different. A foreigner who uses abusive language, flies into a tantrum, criticises another person in public, or just generally loses his cool, will be looked upon not only as socially handicapped or badly brought up, but childishly immature. This means that he or she will run the likely risk of not being taken seriously. Conversely, if someone becomes excessively impatient or angry with you – it does occasionally happen, even with the Lao – keep your dignity and composure, and the other person will lose face. Most people are extremely reluctant to put others in a situation where they lose face as this would reflect on themselves too. Generally speaking, helping others save face is an act of merit and part of the socialisation process.

EXPRESSING EMOTIONS

Open displays of emotions, except at festivals, are rare and emphasis is put on appearing cheerful and level-headed at all times, regardless of one's actual state of mind at the time. Expressions of surprise, anxiety or worry are kept to a minimum, and negative emotions like anger are equated with lack of discipline. The Lao, as anyone who has spent even a few days among them will know, frequently resort to smiling as an expression, not only of happiness and contentment, but as a protective shield for emotions as wide ranging as embarrassment, rage and sadness.

Certain emotions, like fear and worry, are talked about freely but not acted out or displayed in a physical manner. Expressions of surprise or pleasure are usually muted and primarily conveyed through intonation. Foreigners who give Lao friends or staff gifts from time to time, are often heard to make comments like: "And she didn't even say as much as a thank you!" or: "He could at least have opened it in front of us and shown a bit of interest, even if he didn't like it." Opening presents in front of the giver or expressing pleasure on receiving a present is not a common practice among the Lao. To do so would imply greed or over anxiousness to see what is inside. Neither is it seen as absolutely necessary to thank someone on the spot or send them a letter of appreciation, which is often the convention in other countries. Gift giving creates an obligation which will be repaid in some form or the other in the future.

BODY LANGUAGE

In general, the Lao dislike being touched, although handshaking between men is becoming more common. Women, on the whole, still tend to shrink from engaging in even the limp and rather lifeless handshake which is occasionally proffered, preferring to stick with the safer, more courtly Lao *nop*. Spontaneous reflexive actions in the order of hugging, kissing and back slapping are unequivocally taboo. One Lao maid I knew of, went through what for her was the daily ordeal of being tapped on the elbow by her boss every time he needed to attract her attention. It is especially important for men to refrain from touching women in public, even in the case of a girlfriend or wife. Some allowances are made if both partners are foreigners but in rural areas in particular, this can lead to baffled stares, even a mood of simmering hostility.

HEAD, HANDS AND FEET

There are three areas of the body which the Lao are especially sensitive about. These are, in descending order, the head, the hands and the feet.

The head should never be touched, even in jest. The head is the most revered part of the body, and even in the case of a child you would never, for example, ruffle his or her hair in order to show affection or amused appreciation of something. This partly explains why people meeting with Lao of higher rank or social status, like abbots or influential government officials, try their best to keep their heads at a lower level, even if it leads to excruciating spasms of cramp. If you are taller than an approaching monk for example, it is good form to bend when passing him.

Pointing with the forefinger, especially at people, is deemed uncouth, though it is sometimes unavoidable. The same applies to giving or receiving things with the left hand. Gifts are best accepted with a gracious unfolding of both hands. The feet are the lowest part of the body and treated accordingly. You should never point with your feet or sit with the sole of your shoe facing someone. If you are sitting on the floor you should try to keep your feet tucked under you. Women are not expected to sit cross-legged, but if you are a man and do so, spare a thought about which direction the underside of your feet are aimed at. Obviously it would be unthinkable to place your feet on a desk or table top in the company of a Lao person. Many an unfortunate samlor driver has had to put up with the indignity of a passenger's feet placed on the grill behind his back, or worse!

As a general rule it is not good manners to step over another person's feet or body if they are lying down. This is easier said than done when you are trying to alight from a jam packed bus or cross the deck of a Mekong ferry boat strewn with dozens of supine passengers!

REQUESTS AND REFUSALS

Direct requests, except in the case of a shopkeeper whose duty it is to serve the customer, are rare in Laos. More precisely, they are implicit rather than explicit. This particularly applies in the case of requests from young people or subordinates to older folk or person's of higher rank. In such cases, the speaker is more likely to list the reasons for making the request itself. If a young person would like to ask an older person to type out a letter for him, for example, he might start out by saying that a letter needs typing and then add that he cannot type, and so on.

Older people on the other hand, tend to issue commands rather than requests to younger people. The difference between commands and requests is made by the choice of the correct pronoun, and by changing the intonation of the word *nair* (please) from a short, falling tone (the command) to a long, rising one (the request).

The degree to which a person is able to refuse something will depend on the level of friendship or obligation that exists between the two parties. If a close friend, member of the family or benefactor of some kind requests a favour, it is very difficult to refuse directly without appearing to be extremely impolite. In a situation like this the request will neither be accepted or refused, but discussed in such a way as to indicate acceptance or refusal. A person may explain that he is not experienced or qualified enough to undertake the task, or avoid making concrete arrangements and suggest deferring the discussion to a later date. Direct refusals can lead to loss of face, so clearly understood strategies like this are invaluable.

ATTENDING A WEDDING

You are quite likely during the course of your stay in Laos to be invited to attend at least one wedding. Some people are nervous about accepting invitations of this sort on the grounds that, as potentially blundering and ever conspicuous foreigners, they are at risk of upstaging the happy couple. Although customs vary considerably within Laos, especially among the hill tribes, follow the example of the other Lao guests and you can't really go wrong. There aren't in fact, that many customs that you can break. Just remember *not* to kiss the bride!

Among a small but growing middle and upper middle class, it is becoming fashionable to hold wedding receptions at hotels with the trappings and trimmings of a Western style celebration – champagne, designer wedding gowns, tuxedos, an iced and tiered cake and the services of a professional photographer. Usually though, weddings are held at home. The first step in attending a typical Lao wedding is when you receive a colourful, scented invitation card. Guests should place a sum of money – US$20 seems to be the going rate for foreigners, 1000 kip for Lao – in an envelope. When you arrive at the wedding venue you will see a large silver bowl at the entrance which is for placing this money gift. At this point someone will hand you a thimble-sized glass of *lao lao* , a strong rice wine concoction, or possibly a glass of something like Mekong whisky, which you should knock back in one go. Women can refuse these potent brews without causing offence. There are few formalities like speeches and toasts at a Lao wedding. The main event is a large dinner spread, after which the bride and groom will take to the floor for a dance. A *baci* (see Chapter Seven) is usually held in the morning for family members and close friends.

You should ask beforehand to find out if there are likely to be any deviations from the norm, what guests will be wearing and so on. Again, if you are sitting on the floor at any time during the reception, watch out for those feet, and if someone offers you a chair to sit on out of politeness, make sure that it doesn't raise your head up to a higher elevation than an attending monk or elderly person.

DRESS AND CLEANLINESS

It is to the great credit of the Lao that, despite being members of a nation which ranks as one of the ten poorest in the world, their attention to personal hygiene and dress is often far superior to that of many foreigners, particularly tourists and backpackers who can sometimes be remarkably insensitive on this subject, a hangover no doubt, from the sixties when it was *de rigeur* to look unkempt.

Foreigners who walk around decked out like urchins and beggars should not complain if the Lao shy away from forming contacts with them, or if the celebrated Lao smile loses some of its lustre. Attention should also be paid to body odours, especially if you are working or trying to socialise with the Lao. Its not always easy of course, to stifle body odours in the tropics. If you can't keep things under control then shop around for some light perfumes or sprays.

Being clean is strongly associated in the Lao mind with feeling comfortable and relaxed. When you visit a Lao home for example, it is the custom to take your shoes off at the entrance and to be offered the use of the shower room or its equivalent. Your Lao friends are not passing judgment on your personal state of hygiene, but merely fulfilling their role as good hosts eager to make you feel at home.

BIRTH, MARRIAGE AND BEREAVEMENT

The naming ceremony of a newborn child is the first big event in a Lao person's life. A *baci* in which rolls of money are attached to the infant's arms, is held for family members, friends and neighbours or, if in a rural environment, the entire village. The size of the feast and then preparations involved will depend upon the wealth of the family. A bonze will be asked to choose a name for the child, one that will depend upon the astrological conditions at the time.

The next most important ceremony in a boy's life is the one which marks his transition from childhood to adulthood. The manhood ceremony usually takes place around the age of 13, a ritual involving the cutting of the subjects hair to which only close relatives and immediate family are invited as a rule. As a symbol of manhood in more traditional villages, boys still occasionally receive a tattoo which has the added value of warding off evil spirits.

It has long been the custom in Laos for boys to enter the *sangha* (Buddhist clergy) to serve for a brief period as a monk, a practice that has dropped off in the last two or three decades but which, with the present revival of the faith is showing signs of regaining some of its former importance.

Most Lao men marry while they are in their twenties. Brides are usually younger, often in their teens. Young people are free to choose their own partners but families usually have some say in deciding when and where the couple will marry. In more traditional villages a bride-price is paid to the girl's parents. These days this is more likely to be in hard currency. Not so long ago this would have been in grain or livestock.

The divorce rate in Laos is relatively low, partly because marriage is an alliance of two extended families that concerns more than just the couple, but also because a readiness to compromise or to sit down and try to work things out is the characteristic Lao response to almost every situation in which conflict arises.

A young woman dressed in the traditional pha sin *wraparound skirt and the* pha biang, *a silk shawl.*

The final and most important ceremony for a Lao is his funeral. The ministrations of bonzes at funerals is mandatory and more marked than for baptism or marriage. They are involved in almost every stage of the elaborate ceremonies right up to the final cremation. After the body has been prepared, it is placed in a coffin and private family rituals are held. Expressions of grief are kept to a minimum as the Lao firmly believe that displays of sadness retard the rebirth of the spirit of the deceased into a better existence, one step closer to the final goal of nirvana. The entire proceedings, at least from the Western point of view, are surprisingly upbeat. The monks assure the spirits of the deceased that their family mebers are aware of his good fortune in being liberated from the suffering of this life and that they await their own turn with patience and joy. "They are happy without you," the bonzes intone in Pali, "follow then your own destiny!"

The family rites over, the body is placed in a shelter in the garden or yard, a series of feasts and ceremonies begin and guests who knew the deceased troop through partaking of food and drink and cheerfully recounting anecdotes and memories of the departed. The body is finally taken to its cremation pyre on a river bank or in a field, washed and exposed to the sky and then, after everyone has thrown a piece of burning wood on the corpse, left to be consumed. The feasting begins again at this point, along with more comments about the virtues of the deceased.

Families who cannot afford these elaborate rituals must resort to a simple burial in the forest. Graves are left unmarked in such cases, and it is hoped that all trace of the burial spot will vanish as quickly as possible, otherwise the spirit of the dead person runs the risk of joining the malevolent *phi phetu*, spirits known to harass villages and travellers in remote areas.

THE PI MAI FESTIVAL

Few events evoke the life and customs of the Lao better than the Pi Mai, or New Year festival. The Pi Mai is known in Laos as the Fifth Month Festival. In deciding to delay the beginning of the official year by several months, the Lao *horas* (astrologers) intended to place the New Year under more favourable conditions. By beginning the year in April, the Lao have devised a way of making the start of the annual cycle coincide with a renewal of nature.

Luang Prabang is the best place to be over this six day holiday. The festival begins with an interesting market along Thanon Phothisarat, the main street, which is also attended by a number of visiting hill tribes. The afternoon's proceedings move to the west bank of the Mekong where the first day of Pi Mai is celebrated with the building of sand *stupas* which are decorated with astral flags, flowers and candles. The Lao are a pious people but rarely a sanctimonious one: accordingly, although prayers will be staged around the stupas, there is nothing solemn about this part of the festival and the spirited Lao indulge freely in the custom of soaking passersby with buckets of brackish Mekong water. Celebrants fling handfuls of lime powder over themselves or anyone who happens to be passing by, middle-

Water ablutions for passing monks at the Pi Mai festival.

137

aged women dance a slow *lamvong* to the accompaniment of hand cymbals while others paint their faces in lurid colours and engage in playful versions of Lao boxing. Men dressed as hermaphrodites and buffoons roam up and down the sandy shore making grotesque facial expressions at strangers who respond with more water ablutions. As the crowds thicken and the imbibing of *lao lao* becomes more earnest, the antics grow wilder. After an hour or two, the neatly dressed Lao begin to resemble loud, mud-caked versions of their milder, deferential selves.

On the second day of Pi Mai, the town's most venerated monks and abbots head a parade, closely followed by musicians and trance sword dancers. Two lines of women, dressed in the Indianised costumes and gold helmets of the Ramayana tale, lead a parade headed by a beauty queen, Miss Luang Prabang, elected the night before, a procedure which is repeated on yet another day of the festival.

In addition to the propulsive energy, water dousing, circle dancing and good natured drunkenness, the Pi Mai has another side. This consists in the washing of Buddha figures, visits to holy sites and the collecting of plumeria blossoms to adorn the eaves of houses freshly painted for the occasion, or to be placed at the feet of sacred images. On the last day of the festival, the Phra Bang (see Chapter Two) is washed with lustral water and displayed to the crowds at Wat Mai. Here in Luang Prabang, the most quintessentially Lao of all cities, both resident and visitor can come a little closer to understanding the extent to which the Lao cherish their culture, and why.

Chapter Nine

A TASTE OF THE COUNTRY

To eat while it is hot;
Dance whenever one likes.

—A Lao Proverb

"The problem with Laos," a Japanese economist writes, "is that it is neither an industrial nor agricultural economy." Maybe so, but with over 80% of the population engaged in some form of food production, the Lao are unquestionably a nation of agronomists, albeit small time ones.

Few races know their food better than the Lao who are familiar with every step in the food chain. Almost everyone owning a patch of land cultivates their own kitchen gardens, sows a little rice or raises a hen or two. Blessed with the green fingers that come of necessity, most Lao rank as subsistence farmers. Their work is everywhere to be seen. In the dry season for example, sandbanks that emerge mid-stream or along the banks of the Mekong river, are promptly requisitioned as temporary kitchen gardens, producing, within a few short weeks, mouth watering tomatoes, beans and squashes. The Lao certainly know a thing or two about gardening, a skill they are only too pleased to impart to the curious.

A housekeeper or gardener, if you have one, is quite likely to suggest starting up a kitchen garden of this sort in your back yard. This you should eagerly agree too. In a world that leans heavily on chemical fertilisers and pesticides, the fruit and vegetables grown on home plots can taste like rare and exotic foods.

LEARN FROM THE LAO

Shopping for food is done on a daily basis in Laos, as it is in most Asian countries, including the so-called advanced ones like Japan. The storage of large quantities of food remains an alien concept for most people, an idea best suited to cooler climes. Food is bought for immediate use. If you are squeamish about buying live food, you had better have someone else shop for you, or adopt a vegetarian diet, not a bad option in plant rich Laos. Scrambling poultry, and flapping fish are the norm in the wet markets here.

An observer visit to the morning market, the *tha-laht,* or one of the fruit and vegetable affairs that spring up outside temples and along the Mekong, is time well spent. Watch how they squeeze vegetables, smell and prod the products to see how fresh they are. When you see that this is the norm you will be less inhibited about doing the same yourself. Prices, especially for fruit and vegetables, are seldom marked, bargaining and price adjustment are the standard practices.

Markets open from as early as 4.30 a.m. when fresh goods – fruit, vegetables, fish and meat – are sold. Cooked food is sold mainly in the afternoon, and because it is relatively cheap, it is common for the Lao to either eat at the covered restaurant attached to the market or take prepared food straight home.

The slow urbanisation of Lao cities may be changing the face of centres like Vientiane and Savannakhet, but provincial shopping habits still prevail. Food shopping in fact, is a social custom, the

Rice remains the main food staple of Laos.

setting for a convivial exchange of pleasantries which is encouraged by a lack of refrigerated shopping malls, and impersonal department stores, and – good news for gastronomes – a welcome absence of fast food chains.

Provisions like rice, noodles and dried milk are usually bought at small lockup shops, often run by Chinese families who live upstairs on the same premises. If you are satisfied with what you are getting, it makes sense to patronise the same shops and stalls as regular customers are routinely offered a low price without having to bargain for it.

KNOW YOUR FOOD

Few Lao have experienced chronic hunger except perhaps, in wartime or in remote country areas where crops have failed, but existence in what the United Nations has designated the 10th poorest country in the world, has never been taken for granted. A consciousness of food and an evident pleasure in it's taking, are well to the fore in Laos.

Even a cursory glance at one of the language primers for students of Lao reveal what might seem to a foreigner, an inordinate amount of words and phrases connected to the cultivation and preparation of food, such as 'What vegetables do you raise?' and 'The rice is now harvested so we can plant our string beans.' For the Lao, nothing could be more natural than preoccupations of this sort.

In Laos, as elsewhere in Southeast Asia, the place assigned to rice is an important one. Rice, like bread in Western countries, is more than just food. It is a symbol of life. Providing that crops hold out, the Lao generally enjoy a sufficiency in rice, but it is a more precious staple to them than their neighbours like the Vietnamese and Thai with their rich rice deltas. The words for 'hunger' and 'thirsty' in Lao, by the way, translate literally as 'hunger for rice,' and 'hunger for water.' The Lao distinguish between normal rice *(kao)* and the preferred sticky variety *(kao-neo)* which is usually served in communal bowls at home. When there are guests, individual wicker baskets are placed beside your plate.

The same procedure happens in a restaurant. The convention is to knead and roll the rice in your hand until it becomes a firm ball, and then use it as you would a piece of bread.

Cooking is usually done over a charcoal brazier. Refrigerators have begun appearing in Vientiane's large Morning Market but remain almost unheard of in most Lao houses.

ETIQUETTE OF EATING

Food is traditionally eaten with the hands, although when dishes are served with ordinary white rice a spoon and fork is used. Chopsticks *(mai thuu)* are usually only used for eating Chinese style food. Lao restaurants can usually be recognised by the presence of a basin of water standing on a bench or stall outside the entrance. This is used for washing hands before entering. Eating is considered a communal activity; dining alone is regarded as highly unusual, although foreigners, who are regarded as somewhat offbeat anyway, are generally exempted from this judgment, unless they are known to be resident in the country, in which case they may be gently inveighed to be more sociable!

POPULAR CUISINE

Lao cuisine bears a striking resemblance to that of its neighbour Thailand with it's use of fresh vegetables with most of it's meat, poultry and fish dishes. For ordinary people fish, rather than meat, provides their main source of animal protein with the average national consumption running at over seven kilograms per person per annum, the amount in Vientiane district being double that. With no access to the sea, fresh water fishing is of paramount importance, a fact that explains why many Lao react strongly to ideas by their riparian neighbours to build massive dams on the Mekong and it's tributaries.

Fermented fish mixtures like *nam pa* – a thick paste made by filtering water through salted and dried fish – are used extensively to flavour and conserve various kinds of food. They strongly influence the taste of dishes which are often modified with the addition of lemon grass, lime juice and herbs such as coriander leaf. With the ever present side dish of fresh chillies floating in saucers of hot pepper sauce, you can be guaranteed that what you are eating will have a piquancy equal to brimstone and fire.

Lao cuisine is less influenced by Chinese cooking than the dishes of some of it's neighbours. The mixture of sweet and acidic tastes is not that popular. Chilly and red pepper dominate the soups and sauces of the Lao table but there is also a liberal use made of herbs. The Lao are never far from their forests with their wealth of edible plants like mint, water lily stems, fennel, marguerita leaves and aromatic water plants. They are there to refresh the eye just as much as the palate.

There are sweet desserts too, most of which eschew the Western use of flour, butter and milk. Thin tissues of beaten egg stewed in boiling syrup, lotus flowers doused in coconut milk, and a sweet cheese made from mangos, are consumed in private homes but are usually more difficult to sample in restaurants.

People interested in learning the finer points of Lao cooking should watch out for notices advertising cooking courses that sometimes get posted on the boards of foreign clubs or international schools, or in the pages of publications like the *Vientiane Times*. The Women's International Group are also a good source of information on this and many other subjects of interest and use to the expatriate in Laos.

MORE FISH TALK

In landlocked Laos the Mekong and its tributaries are the main source for culinary invention. Freshwater catches, limited in scope, are enhanced with herbs, organic moulds and acidulous sauces that offer flavours new to most visitors. The roe of a giant and somewhat endangered fish called *pa boeuk*, indigenous to this lower Mekong basin region, adds, along with other mortared, marinated or broiled dishes, a special distinction to Lao cuisine.

To overcome the dependence on season and availability, the Lao resort to preserving much of their food. Pickling brine is used to preserve whole fish. Fish acidulated with fermented rice is pounded to become a moist and flavoursome compound called *sompa*. The same method is used to preserve pork and buffalo.

Fish is by no means the only dish found on the Laotian table though it is the most common. The national dish, if such a thing exists, must surely be *lap,* the Laotian version of steak tartare, a traditional party dish. Finely minced venison or beef – buffalo will do as second best – are prepared with seasonings and fresh herbs. *Phaneng kay*, a chicken dish in which the bird is stuffed with ground peanuts and stewed in coconut milk, also ranks fairly high in the meat hierarchy, with strips of dried buffalo and stuffed frogs holding a lower, but not despised, place in Lao esteem.

Traditional foods offered as alms to monks at certain times of the year such as the days after the Buddhist Lent, and routinely consumed in homes throughout the month, include ubiquitous amounts of sticky rice, sugar-cane buds, areca, boiled and spicy chicken, tubers of all kinds, cassava, and a potent Lao version of moonshine, *lao-lau*, made from rice. Minced dishes sweetened with a pinch of sugar to bind them are flavoured with more herbs.

A Laotian meal is incomplete without soup which is usually served in the middle or end of a meal, never at the beginning. Some of the most delicious are made from common vegetables like bamboo shoots and stick-beans. Vegetables, except in the case of *gnam gnuan,* a kind of Lebanese chopped salad, are rarely served as a separate dish, but are added to a communality of ingredients with interacting flavours. Eggs, which are precious, make rare appearances in occasional preparations like *phan khay,* thin pancakes stuffed with raw meat, wrapped in banana leaves and steamed.

TIME HONOURED COOKING METHODS

Traditionally, much of the cooking has been done without the benefit of conventional utensils. Large fish, for example, are stuffed with herbs and then wrapped and tied in the bark of the banana tree before being buried in the red-hot ashes of a fire. Patience is required for this kind of cooking, but the end result, a slow-roasted fish deliciously enhanced by the hint of sap, out-matches the capacity of any oven.

These time-honoured methods of cooking are not only effective in producing food of outstanding gourmet quality, but are also ecologically sound. Cleaning a fish, filling it with condiments and then coating it with moist clay before consigning it to the hot ashes, will produce not only a rustic, aromatic taste, and be entirely biodegradable, but will also save you from scouring scales as they simply peel off the fish the moment the mould is removed. The same casket method of cooking is used for steaming fish that has been filleted, then pounded with coconut milk, a dish known as *ho mok pa fok.*

The criteria for judging the quality of Lao food lies in the level of finesse achieved in the preparation of purees, the balance and dominance of one herb over another – galangal over ginger, carambola over southernwood, and so on. Other important aspects of preparation include the pounding and mincing of the meat and fish, and the skill in handling the mode of cooking, be it charcoal, ash wood, steam or earthenware.

Traditionally in wealthy families, the best dishes were never prepared by servants but by the mistress of the house, using the simplest of instruments – long knives, small mortars and a chopping board (usually a segment of a tree trunk.) As a mark of hospitality and largesse, tradition still dictates that more places should be set than the actual number of guests expected.

THE RESTAURANT SCENE

"Homesickness," Che Guevara once noted, "begins with food." How true! Sooner or later the novelty of foreign food, however enticing, can begin to wear off, giving rise to spectral images of a juicy porterhouse steak, plate of sushi, waffles floating in honey, or whatever it is you most associate with home.

Fortunately, in places like Vientiane and Luang Prabang, the last couple of years have seen a long-awaited flowering of reasonably priced, good quality restaurants, serving both Lao and international cuisine. Compared to only a couple of years ago, expats can now be said to be rather spoilt for choice. Some of the best are French and French run.

The French Legacy

The Lao may have risen against their French colonial masters but a pervasive gastronomic legacy endures. It's presence is seen in the pyramids of baguettes sold in the morning markets, at bus stations and near public buildings. The Lao fill these baguette sandwiches with a pate and onion mixture and call them *khao jii pate*. French bread is also eaten with fried eggs or dipped plain into hot milk coffee *(Ka feh nom hawn)*. Croissants are usually available in the tasty bakeries of Vientiane also but, like baguettes, may be a little more difficult to find the further you get from Lao cities, where bread ovens are almost unheard of.

WHAT YOU SEE IS WHAT YOU GET

One of the pleasures of tropical Southeast Asian countries is eating al fresco. Nothing is concealed from the eyes of the customer. These open-plan, kitchen-restaurants are usually found clustering around the morning and night markets, or are set up at roadsides and junctions.

Perhaps because journeys by road tend to take an eternity, bus stations, garages, forks in the road or the boarding points for chain ferries across rivers, also boast plenty of basic, culinary choices from fresh fruit, sachets of cooked rice to grasshoppers roasted on a spit.

The Mekong river provides the Lao not only with their most vital transportation link but with a scenic, aquatic playground. All of the country's major towns are built on this waterway. Stroll along it's banks and sooner or later you will come across a restaurant or bar with a good sunset view and perhaps, a beer garden.

Baguettes, one of the more popular features of the French legacy.

Almost every town has it's own night market and nearby noodle shop. Menus in English, or any other language come to that, are virtually unheard of, but the style of eating obviates the need for such sophisticated adjuncts. Inspecting the ingredients and pointing is usually enough to get you a decent custom mix, a bit of everything. Failing that, you could ask for the *ahanphi-set*, which means 'special food.'

Slightly more upmarket than the street and public stalls are the so-called 'eat-and-drink' shops *(han kin deum)* which often serve Chinese and Vietnamese food and chalk their menus up on a blackboard on the wall.

These eateries are augmented by a great number of ambulants, portable food barrows that get pushed around the street, the theory being that if you keep moving you don't need a license.

EATING IN A LAO HOME

Visitors to Lao households are never offered food or drink. It is provided automatically after the guest has been asked, 'have you eaten?' It is expected that the guest will give a negative answer, after which he or she will be included in the family meal or, if they have already eaten, served the same meal, even if this involves cooking again. In the likelihood that you strike up a few good Lao friends, it is quite normal for the visitor to nominate what he wants to eat. Naturally enough, people with a reputation as good cooks, seem to have an inordinate number of friends popping in conveniently around meal times! If you don't want to be eaten out of home, you had better keep your culinary skills a secret!

Dishes are often laid out on a long strip of cloth set on the floor or table. You can help yourself to whatever tempts you. There are no set rules governing the order in which you should help yourself to dishes. Neither are there mandatory preliminaries to meals of this kind which are usually relaxed and informal affairs. If you show too much of a tendency to hold back in fact, your hosts are likely to jokingly reproach you for 'behaving like a son-in-law.' When you have eaten enough it is polite manners to place the lid on the top of your rice basket. Failure to do so is held by the more superstitious to presage a divorce in the family within a year.

DARING FOOD

Are there any real limits for the truly adventurous expat gastronome? That rather depends on you. Discrimination in food is not a question of prejudice but of taste. The more open-minded foreigner will usually be able to transform an antipathy for a dish into a relish for it. But how about *luk-andong,* a traditional northern dish in which a swallow is wrapped in banana leaves and then left to rot for a week or so before cooking, a process that it would be flattering to call marination.

Other foods which expats may find alarming at first, but which the Lao consider just plain ordinary, include pork offal, dried water-buffalo rind, and special treats like pounded onion and heart, cow's placenta and baked moose. Perhaps it's just the idiosyncrasies of Lao-English, but don't be surprised to find dishes such as 'small intestine salad and hormones' appearing on restaurant menus.

Durian fruit is highly regarded in Laos as it is elsewhere in Southeast Asia. Most foreigners dislike this giant fruit. This is a pity: in season, ripe durians can be bought from roadside vendors for as little as 50 cents US. If you like food that is at all off the beaten digestive track, you may come after a spell in Laos, to acquire a liking for these offerings.

HAZARDS

The same precautions apply to Laos as to most Southeast Asian or tropical countries. New arrivals should try to maintain a balanced diet which contains at least some of the familiar elements your tummy recalls from it's former home. Protein is easily and safely obtained from tofu, lentils, nuts, beans and eggs, all of which are relatively easy

A market vendor on the Mekong spreads her wares on the floor.

to come by in Laos. Fruit that can be peeled is a reliable source of vitamins. Roughage and grain in the form of bread and rice is important too. Local meat and fish must be well cooked, otherwise there is a serious risk of parasitic invasion. Despite what people may tell you, freezing or marinating food does not kill these organisms. Rinsing and soaking vegetables for 20 minutes in a tincture of iodine is common practice among expatriate families, especially those who are taking extra precautions because of children. An alternative to the rather strong smell of iodine is Clorox, a very effective mixture which is available locally.

Water should never be drunk from the tap, whatever your landlord says. Nor should it be drunk unboiled. The best rule of thumb when contemplating using ice is, don't! This is a harsh rule to follow in the tropics though, and one that sooner or later, most people lapse from. Chipped ice is the one to look out for as it probably comes from a large block of ice that has come into contact with all manner of bacteria on it's trip from the factory. Ice cubes made from purified water, are delivered in sealed plastic bags and deemed safer if you must cool down your Coke or lime juice with something.

Bear these simple precautions in mind and you will be able, at the end of a meal, to pronounce a heartfelt *Saep lai!*, ("That was delicious") rather than a premonitious *Baw suh-bye!*, ("I think I am going to be ill!") Bon Appetite!

Chapter Ten

GETTING THINGS DONE

Europeans who come here to live, soon acquire a certain recognisable manner. They develop quiet voices, and gentle, rapt expressions.

—*A Dragon Apparent,* Norman Lewis

Yes, there are still quite a few 'rapt' looking foreign residents of the kind noted by Norman Lewis back in the early 1950s, but they are not only Europeans these days. Living among courteous, and generally pacific people such as the Lao, is bound to have an effect on impressionable visitors. "Some of the least urgent souls on earth," is how another writer described the Lao. Even some of the most driven of people have been known to throw in the corporate towel and be discovered after a few days in the country, wandering sockless and fancy-free among the green temples of Vientiane or Luang Prabang, or at a riverside bar soaking up one of the Mekong's Technicolor sunsets, all pretence of work abandoned.

The transition from euphoria to feet planted squarely on terra firma, is where culture shock can begin. The impact of relocating to a foreign country and changing a whole lifestyle in the process, is often delayed. The realities of living in a developing country especially, can come as quite a shock. One way to overcome or cope with the three common stages of euphoria, disenchantment and adjustment in the busy early weeks of living in Laos is to concentrate on getting things done.

EDUCATION

If you are arriving in Lao with a family, one of your immediate priorities will be getting your children into the right school as soon as possible. The only schools to which foreign children are eligible, and probably the only ones you would consider putting them in anyway, are located in Vientiane. Your embassy or consulate will be able to supply you with a list of names and addresses but you should also ask around the resident foreign community before making any decisions.

There are various small but well run institutions from preschool, kindergarten and primary, up to secondary level. A number of different kinds of coeducational schools exist, from state-run to private and non-profit making organisations. Many run standard curriculums, others may have special resources like language laboratories, or courses in computer literacy, or teaching systems like the Montessori method, so spend some time shopping around and visiting schools. The main languages of instruction are Lao, English, French, Swedish and Russian. Several schools run bilingual curriculums.

External correspondence courses for both children and adults can be studied from home but you should try if possible, to arrange these before coming to Laos. Materials are also best bought beforehand. There are also private lessons available in piano, ballet, the Lao language (see Chapter Five), office and management skills and computer usage.

HEALTH CARE AND CLINICS

The first priority when living in the tropics is to stay healthy. Illness will immediately throw a spanner in the works, and all your best laid schemes and plans will grind to a sudden halt. The roster of possible ailments and diseases you could contract in Laos is truly formidable. Included among the most common are malaria, fungal infections, internal parasites, hepatitis, Japanese encephalitis, dengue fever and bouts of conjunctivitis. And that's just for starters!

If a few sensible precautions are taken however, most people manage to avoid the nastier forms of illness. Hygiene really begins at home where special attention should be taken in the preparation of food and in the use of drinking water (see Chapter Nine). Try to impress any Lao staff you might have with the importance of sanitary food preparation. Diarrhoea, hepatitis A and dysentery are among the common intestinal disorders that can be transmitted through infected food or water. Malaria is endemic in Laos where it is said that up to one-third of the population at one time or another, come down with malarial bouts. Although there is no malaria in cities like Vientiane and Luang Prabang, the radius of invulnerability is small, and anybody intending to travel far should consult a clinic for advice on suitable precautions before setting off, although there is no absolute deterrent against every strain of malaria, many of which have developed a resistance to drugs of this sort. Ultimately, a good insect repellent may be more useful than anything else. Early evening and night are when squads of mosquitoes usually appear, so try to wear long sleeved shirts and long trousers or slacks. Dark clothes and perfume are known to attract mosquitoes. Useful precautions at home include electric fans or air-conditioning, mosquito nets for sleeping and screens at the window. Mosquito coils should not be overused as they have detrimental effects on health, but may be indispensable for upcountry trips.

Stay well clear of stray animals, including other people's pets, even if it means giving offence to their proud owners. Rabies is

155

usually transmitted by a bite, but the virus can also infect people by a simple tick entering the body through a split or opening in the skin. Hepatitis A and B are also infectious diseases. Hepatitis A is usually contracted through contaminated food, eating utensils or water. Hepatitis B may be contracted from infected needles. These include those used by acupuncturists and tattooists. Even if you intend to have your ears pierced, make sure that needles are properly sterilised. Supervision in general, seems to be one of the keys to good health in Laos.

Most foreigners will experience some adjustment symptoms in their first days or weeks in Laos, your body's own version of culture shock. Depending upon your situation, your various biological clocks will need time to recover from jet lag, changes in diet and the impact of a tropical climate, particularly if you arrive during the rainy season. Preventive measures include regular doses of liquids, a drop in alcohol consumption, good, balanced nutrition and a decent night's sleep. Avoid the tropical sun or cut down on its effect by wearing a sun hat and covering your skin in liberal doses of protective cream. Among the tell tale signs that your body is not coping as well as it should do with its new surroundings are headaches, dizziness and listlessness. Heat exhaustion, diarrhoea caused by a change in diet and the invasion of unfamiliar microbes into the body, and prickly heat, an irritating skin rash caused when pores are not releasing perspiration quickly enough, are some of the more common minor health problems incurred by expatriates.

Medical services, even in the capital, are severely limited. The Australian Embassy Clinic, which is open to all nationalities, has a small but highly qualified staff of doctors and nurses who are on 24-hour call for emergencies and can arrange for the transfer of patients requiring special treatment or surgery, to Thailand. The Hospital de l'Amitie, also provides treatment for orthopedic emergencies. They can also give you a list of recommended hospitals and dental clinics in Udon Thani and Bangkok.

There are also one or two qualified people practising alternative, or complementary medicine, such as acupuncture, reflexology, reiki and aromatherapy massage. Pharmacies are plentiful in Vientiane, though they may not always stock what you need. Always check the expiry date before you buy anything and the general condition of pharmaceutical goods as storage conditions may be less than perfect.

PLANNING TRIPS

While you are living in Laos you will surely want to travel around and acquaint yourself with your new host country. When planning a trip there are several local factors to bear in mind. Clothing is important as there are considerable variations in temperature and other weather conditions between different altitudes. Travelling around such a mountainous country will be more unpredictable than you are probably used to. There is no railway system and if you intend to use boats you should allow yourself plenty of extra time. The Mekong is only seasonably navigable, and roads which are not properly surfaced are often impassable during the wet season. Still, where there is a will there is a way and the staff at Lao Aviation or one of the many competent local travel agencies in Vientiane will do all they can to adjust your itinerary to adverse conditions.

The range of accommodation in Laos, from international hotels with faxes, cable TV and room service to humble guest houses with squat toilets, ply board beds and nails driven into the walls to serve as coat hangers, is broad to say the least, but the extent of choice is still quite limited and visitors, especially to the provinces, may find themselves gratefully accepting whatever is offered. The few international or tourist class hotels that exist are often quite expensive by Lao standards. Budget hotels really only exist in large towns. One of the most welcome trends in the tourist business in recent years has been the renovation, usually to very high standard, of old French colonial villas. These offer space, comfort and an elegant setting at an affordable tariff, usually the US$25–60 range. You will find guest houses in most small towns, even in some villages. Always check the room before committing yourself as standards of cleanliness vary considerably. If you are in a remote rural area and all else fails, you can appeal to a villager to convert his home into a temporary bed and breakfast establishment. In all probability they will say yes.

Very often, when travelling in the provinces, you will have no precise idea of what you can expect to find so it is a good idea to prepare a few useful resources such as water purification tablets, and a basic first aid kit containing band aids, antiseptic ointments, aspirins, and so on. You would be surprised at the world of difference a clean set of towels, bed sheets, a mosquito net and a couple of bars of soap can make to your comfort and state of mind. A torch is essential as power failures are an almost everyday occurrence in many areas.

You used to need a special pass to travel from one province to another but these have now been waived. When you travel upcountry or outstation you will need to report to the local police authority checkpoint, show them your passport and pay a few kip for a receipt proving that your presence has been properly noted. If you don't do this you will have to pay a fine when you leave. The checkpoints will be in either the airport or river port, at border points on roads crossing from one province to another or in the local government office, the equivalent of the Town Hall. Needless to say, it is not a good idea to travel with young children in these under serviced and isolated areas of Laos.

ROADS, BOATS AND PLANES

The network of roads, river and air routes for getting around the country look sound enough on paper but often turn out to be unreliable and wildly unpredictable in practice. This is why it is so important before embarking on a journey to check prevailing conditions to establish that you have at least an even chance of arriving on time and in reasonable shape.

The wooden side of the colourfully painted Lao truck-buses that ply many of the country routes.

Consult as many people as possible before setting out on long haul road travel to find out the condition of the surface, whether there have been any recent incidents such as attacks on lone vehicles, natural disasters like landslides or flash floods, or if it would be possible to join a convoy taking the same route. Aid and volunteer groups who travel regularly out into the back of beyond are usually well informed and up to the minute sources. Your embassy will be able to give you an accurate picture of what's going on too. Foreigners should never drive unescorted at night on remote country roads. A number of international funded road projects have already been initiated, so great improvements can be expected over the next few years as Laos acquires properly integrated north-south and east-west routes. The long, formerly gruelling, stretch of Route 13 from Vientiane to

Savannakhet for example, was finished in 1996. Many other roads are under construction.

If you have the time and you enjoy rugged travel – basic sleeping facilities and food which becomes increasingly bland with each day that passes – you can travel all the way from Luang Prabang to Savannakhet by boat. Officially, foreigners need permission to travel in this way, but once given you have quite a bit of latitude as far as deciding on a vessel. You can take one of the larger diesel ferries, join other passengers on a deckless *hua houa leim*, a typical Lao river boat, or even hire an entire boat for yourself. Again, weather conditions, especially during the dry season when sand banks and razor-sharp rocks suddenly surface, should be carefully inquired about before setting off. There are a number of partially navigable Mekong tributaries and other backwaters rarely explored by foreigners or tourists which pass through landscapes of spellbinding beauty.

Scheduled flights exist to most major towns, and also quite a few out of the way destinations in Laos as well. It's actually quite surprising just how far you can go on Lao Aviation's aged but plucky little service. When weather conditions are in your favour, it can also be a rapid and comfortable way to travel. Lao Aviation also fly to Bangkok, Phnom Penh, Ho Chi Minh City and Hanoi. Thai Air have two flights a day to Vientiane, and a relative newcomer, Silk Air, do twice-weekly flights between Singapore and Vientiane.

Scheduled flights are often subject to delays so it is wise to book well in advance. Foreigner's pay double the going rate for locals. If you are paying for a Lao colleague, guide or member of your domestic staff to go with you, you will be charged at the Lao rate for them.

Although one or two new planes have begun to be leased out to the government, the bulk of the domestic fleet is made up of twin-prop Anatovs and 17-seat Y-12s. Spare parts for these Russian and Chinese stalwarts are not always easy to come by these days. If you were ever a closet Biggles fan, here is your chance to experience some of the thrills and spills of early aviation. Chocks away!

CROSSING THE RIVER

If you wish to take your own car across the Mittaphab (Friendship) Bridge into Thailand, you will need to have the necessary papers for both the Lao and Thai authorities each end. Your employer or embassy will be able to help you out with this. Providing you have a valid multiple re-entry visa, you can cross back and forth as often as you like. If you do decide to take a vehicle across you will need an International Driver's Licence and Thai Third Party Insurance. The Thais are quite strict about this.

There is also a shuttle bus across but you will have to wait until it fills up with enough people – a delay of over an hour in some cases – before proceeding. A further wait while you go through the immigration and customs procedure at each end adds to the whole time consuming business. Note that the bridge closes for a two-hour lunch from noon and in the evening at six o'clock.

CLUBS AND INTEREST GROUPS

Joining a club, social circle or special interest group is an excellent way to make friends, acquire a helpful support group and start tapping some of the local wisdom. Several different kinds of group exist, from well established organisations to ad hoc circles set up to satisfy the interests of naturalists, bridge players, amateur historians and the like. In an expat community as relatively small as this it is usually quite easy to seek out people who share mutual interests, although the Californian family I knew whose every moment of spare time was spent shooting the country's white-water rapids, clutching tyre inner tubes, met a certain amount of difficulty persuading friends to join their daredevil escapades!

The Women's International Group (WIG), which also welcomes men, offers one of the best support systems for its members and opportunities to pool interests and learn more about Lao culture, history and current affairs. Its activities reflect the interest of its members but include such things as arts and crafts, cooking courses,

play readings, sports activities and the environment. They also sponsor a number of charity, fund-raising events like bazaars and fashion shows. They also provide openings in the field of volunteer work. Musicians will be able to find groups like choral singing and instrumental societies who are always looking for fresh blood. The Australian Embassy has its own recreation club open to all comers, with leisure activities like film screenings, darts, an excellent pool and special courses in things like aerobics. The Russian Culture Centre offers a relaxed milieu of books, video, chess, musical evenings, lectures as well as a coffee shop.

Sports, health and outdoor activities are plentiful but, you will have to make inquiries. These include basketball, golf, dance, exercise and modern movement classes, softball, squash, tennis, rugby and yoga groups. There are occasional events like triathlons and outdoor excursions put on and an active Hash House Harriers branch in town. Members of the Vientiane Play Group meet every week. It's open to 0–5 year-olds. There are one or two good health centres offering saunas, massage and relaxing plunges into hot baths, that are worth visiting. Some wats in Vientiane offer traditional herbal saunas and massage in a pleasant, open-air setting. Herbal teas are served between trips to the sauna.

RELIGIOUS CENTRES

Apart from the ubiquitous Buddhist wat, foreigners will find a sprinkling of small Roman Catholic, Evangelical, Anglican-Episcopal and interdenominational churches, meeting halls and fellowship centres in both Vientiane and several more provincial towns. Regular Sunday services and bible reading classes are held throughout the year. There is also a Baha'i Faith Centre which offers 'deepening classes' at the weekends. Muslims will find their spiritual home and hearth on Fridays at the local mosque in Vientiane. The resident Imam or Mullah offers lessons in the Koran, and during Ramadan, Taraweh prayers are held every night.

WRITTEN MATERIAL, FILM AND VIDEO

Keeping in touch with the outside world and your own culture is just as important as assimilating things Lao. Residents should stock up on their favourite writers – there's nothing like starting a good novel in one country and finishing it in another – take out all your magazine subscriptions before leaving home, and make sure that children have plenty of familiar as well as new books to comfort and engage them. There are excellent book shops in places like Bangkok, Singapore and Hong Kong but Vientiane, alas, is lamentably under serviced in this respect. The Raintree Bookstore along Thanon Pang Kham is the best bookshop in town with a good selection of new and used titles in English and other languages as well as some magazines. This is also the best place to find books on Laos, although some hotels, mini-marts, souvenir shops and ticket booths at the bigger wats, also sell books of local interest. If you are desperate to get hold of a copy of *Asia Week*, *Popular Mechanics* or *Good Housekeeping*, the Government Book Shop is usually happy to order them for you.

The Australian Embassy Library has over 10,000 titles, mostly in English, and a good selection of magazines and periodicals. The Russians have their equivalent to the Australian Embassy Library at the Russian Cultural Centre Library, which also stocks books in English, French and Lao.

163

Newspapers

The *Bangkok Post* and the *Nation*, two commendable Thai English language newspapers, are readily available in Vientiane. The *KPL Newssheet*, in Lao, French and English, is put out by the government and can be ordered or picked up in hotel lobbies and at embassies. The *Vientiane Times* is a weekly paper in English which you can subscribe to in the provinces as well. *Discover Laos* promotes Lao tourism and is usually available at the beginning of each month. French readers can pick up copies of *Le Mekong*, a monthly paper covering the region. You may also come across the *Passason* and *Vientiane Mai*, the two Lao language dailies.

Cinemas

At the time of writing, the only working cinema in Vientiane features films in Thai, Russian and Indian, although one would think that it is only a matter of time before they start showing English and French films. There are a number of commercial outlets for video hire. Despite the occasional purge by the censors, who seem to follow an unfathomable logic of their own in their selection of what is fit to be seen, many of the films on offer are surprisingly up to date. The quality of the print is not always as good as it could be but is improving steadily. The American Embassy, Russian Culture Centre and Centre de Langue Francaise de Vientiane, all hold regular screenings in their respective languages.

TAPPING THE CULTURE

While discos, taped music and live bands have certainly made an impact in recent years, the contemporary performing arts and general entertainment scene remains fairly tame. It will be a long time before Michael Jackson or the Bolshoi Ballet make it out here, but the performing arts which have survived in Laos are well worth seeing while they still remain relatively untainted.

A musician playing the khene, *the national instrument of Laos.*

Lao music, song and dance, in common with Thailand, is strongly inspired by a mixture of Indian myth and local folklore. Bamboo flutes and various percussive instruments like the *nang nat* – a kind of xylophone – and a falange of suspended bronze cymbals called a *knong vong*, play an important part in the traditional Lao orchestra. The *kaen*, a hand-held, pan-like set of bamboo pipes, is the national instrument. *Seb gnai* orchestras, as they are known, can be occasionally heard during religious ceremonies and at certain festivals. While hotels, beer gardens and the like sometimes put on cultural digests for tourists or their Lao customers, festivals are probably the best times of the year to catch authentic musical recitals, folk dances and performances of the Lao version of the Indian Ramayana dance epic.

Most festivals *(boun)* are moveable, following as they do the Buddhist lunar calendar. There are countless local festivals, performances of the *baci* (see Chapter Seven) and days set aside to honour non-Lao dates like the Chinese New Year. The following is a list, by no means exhaustive, of some of the main events in the festive and honorary calendar.

- **Jan:** New Year's Day (1st). Pathet Lao Day (6th). Army Day (20th). Boun Pha Vet (20th).
- **Feb:** Magha Puja. Chinese New Year.
- **Mar:** Women's Day (8th). People's Party Day (22nd). Boun Khoun Khao. Harvest Festival.
- **Apr:** Boun Pimai.
- **May:** Labour Day. Visakha Busa. Boun Bang Fay.
- **Jun:** Children's Day. Khao Phansa.
- **July:** Start of Awk Phansaa (Buddhist Lent).
- **Aug:** Lao Issara Day. Liberation Day (23rd). Ho Khao Padap Dinh.

Laos is undergoing a gentle revival of the performing arts as visitor numbers steadily increase.

- **Sept:** Bouk ok Phansa.
- **Oct:** Freedom from the French Day (12th). Boun Souang Hena (Water Festival & Boat Races).
- **Nov:** That Luang Festival.
- **Dec:** Hmong New Year. Independence Day.

Chapter Eleven

UPCOUNTRY: ANOTHER CULTURE SHOCK

AN EVEN SMALLER COSMOS

If you thought Vientiane was small and refreshingly out of step with the times, the remote villages and settlements, the locus of rural life that typify the country's remarkably unchanged outlands, are minuscule time capsules, worlds within worlds that very few foreigners have ever seen.

Even the French, who at any one time only had a couple of hundred administrators in the whole country, soon recognised the limits of their influence and effectively gave up trying to implement their *mission civilitrise* on whole areas of the country, particularly the far north, which were left to more or less go their own way. Today, despite the efforts of a central government keen to promote national unity, little seems to have changed at the local village level in the more isolated 'upcountry' areas.

A HANDFUL OF FOREIGNERS

The foreigners you are most likely to bump into in the provinces will often be working in the aid field, for NGO groups or for humanitarian organisations as social workers, project advisers and doctors. You may also come across experts in the field of mineral research and exploration, dam construction, forestry and fisheries, the odd anthropologist and even, from time to time, the occasional intrepid tourist. Whoever you are and whatever you do, as a foreigner, even one from another Asian country, be prepared to stick out like a sore thumb. Forget any plans you might have had of finding anonymity in a rural retreat. You'll have more chance of that in Vientiane than upcountry where even the normally incurious Lao will not fail to note the arrival of a new face.

Unsurfaced roads during the rainy season pose endless transport problems.

169

There are some advantages to living in a community where your identity is public knowledge, however. Theft and other crimes, for example, are quite rare in these areas, and women are seldom at risk from peeping toms or other sexual deviants, though some of the locals may be dismayed to find a foreign women, especially a highly qualified one at that, living in their midst.

Foreigners will certainly find that their presence is noted and commented upon but that generally, the Lao are a non-intrusive people who tend to let others go their own way in the spirit of live and let live. Rural Lao, who are temperamentally averse to any form of commotion or disruption in their lives, except during their festivals when plenty of collective steam is let off, are unlikely to tell you to pipe down if they think you are making too much noise or to be more reserved in manner. You are expected to notice these things yourself and act accordingly. I did however, see the following appeal pinned to the wall of a police office in the remote province of Luang Nampha once, which I reproduce here exactly as I found it.

> Please check your passport with us.
> You must put your dressing polite.
> Don't put on your skirt come to our office.
> And don't say loud. Hope you understand.
> Thank you.

Tranquillity, equanimity and imperturbability are valued above all else, a fairly normal preference among country folk the world over. The difference is that the majority of rural Lao genuinely don't appear to aspire towards an urban lifestyle.

ACCOMMODATION

Most residents spend time upcountry on behalf of the organisation they are working for, so things like accommodation (much cheaper here) housekeeping (usually not necessary) and the supply of hard to come by commodities to live on, will already have been arranged for

A typical upcountry house built on stilts.

you. In many cases, housing will be quite basic and you may find, in the more extreme cases, that the luxury of your fully furnished French villa in the capital or cosy bachelor flat, is exchanged for an earth floor hut, swiftly put together from wattle and pandanus reeds with no running water, except when the local river or stream decides to take a diversion through your main room! Be warned that other intruders such as mice, rats, even snakes, may also take an interest in your home, particularly if there is food lying around. That's one reason many houses in Laos are raised up on stilts.

If you have to arrange your own accommodation things can be a little more difficult. For a start, there are no flats and habitable houses ready to go are few and far between. Many foreigners resort to lodging with other colleagues, if there are any that is in the posting that you have been allotted. Boarding with a Lao family or putting up at whatever passes for the equivalent of the local guest house are other options.

Lodging

Many families will be only too happy to earn a little extra hard currency by taking in a lodger. It's a good way to improve your Lao – so too is living upcountry in general, where few very few locals will speak your language – and the family, if you do your best to observe their house rules, may prove to be a good contact if and when you return to the area in the future. If you do decide to stay with a family and manage to get your own room, you'll have to get used to a different concept of privacy. Unlike Muslim or Hindu families however, where there may be food and dress taboos to closely avoid even at home, Lao households are fairly relaxed. Few of them, and this also applies to the more rustic kind of guest house, will have running water. The Lao are just as mindful of personal hygiene as most other Southeast Asians, and provision, in the form of large storage jars, usually placed in the open or under a small, roofed enclosure, are found in most Lao back yards. Members of the family take it in turn to strip down to shorts or a firmly knotted towel, and then slosh pailfuls of water over themselves. Complete nudity, except in the case of children, is not usual. In villages located in jungle or mountain areas, a communal well may serve the same end. You'll often see people bathing in rivers, even in quite large towns. If you ever bathe

or swim in this way make sure its in fairly deep, running water where there is less risk of parasitic invasion. Most toilets, where they exist, will be the squat variety which the British call 'continental toilets' and the people on the continent call 'Arab toilets!' Otherwise, it's a furtive stroll to the nearest bit of vegetation.

Bathing in the Mekong or one of its numerous tributaries is one practice foreigners are not advised to follow.

Don't overburden the family with visits by friends at all hours of the day. Coping with one foreigner at a time and striving for that much lauded ideal of harmony will be quite enough for most families to begin with. The Lao are a congenitally shy and reserved people so you should be ultra-sensitive to the fact that the family may be too polite to mention that you are doing something to disrupt the household.

Familiarise yourself with the way things work and the way the household is run so that you don't have to keep asking how to change the wicks on the pressure lamps, where the rubbish is disposed or how to get the stove started. In many houses there will be no gas ranges for cooking. This will be done at an open charcoal brazier.

There may be strong disparities between the range and quality of the food you have been used to eating back in the city and what the family you are staying with are used to serving. If you find the food too monotonous you will have to make a work related excuse to avoid offence and arrange to have your meals at a friends house or in the marginally better local restaurant.

DRESS AND CONDUCT

The more remote an area is the more conservative it becomes is only true up to a point. What is considered the standard dress code for women of the Ippo fraternity, for example – short skirts, woolly leggings, bare shoulders and heaps of silver accessories – might, seen through the prism of Western dress codes, be considered quite fashionable, daring even. When visiting the villages of ethnic minorities, whatever you wear will arouse a certain amount of interest, if only in the quality, colour and cut of the cloth. As values are so totally different in the really remote areas, as long as you dress conservatively, you are unlikely to give offence.

As far as provincial towns go, men won't have many problems fitting in with jeans, flannels or a locally bought safari suit, or the floppy shorts that everyone seems to wear in the hotter weather. Women – forever condemned wherever they go to pay more attention to these matters – should follow that tiresome maxim, 'When in doubt, cover up!' Sensible clothing for the hot low and middle elevations and the cool, occasionally genuinely cold, higher climes should be packed as field work often involves unpredictable changes of altitude.

Being prepared for the unpredictable is part and parcel of the upcountry experience. Some basic survival skills like being able to change a flat tyre, apply first aid and start a campfire may come in handy at unexpected times. Even more vital for this kind of lifestyle, however temporary, are the virtues of patience, a sympathy for the local culture and a good sense of humour.

Opium addiction in the outlying provinces, particularly of the notorious Golden Triangle, is alarmingly high.

175

Chapter Twelve

MAKING CONNECTIONS

"Whatever speed the rest of the world may travel, the Laotians are never in a hurry."

—*Temples and Elephants,* Carl Bock, 1884

Foreigners who quip that the designation LAO PDR actually stands for 'Please Don't Rush,' are making an affectionate, though occasionally exasperated, comment, not an unkind one. Mistakes may be minimal in the Lao business world, but delays are another thing. To quote a well known piece of folk wisdom, a Lao proverb in this case: 'You don't have to feed the baby until it cries.' Here is an attitude which residents soon become familiar with. Unless something is urgent, why address it now?

There are several good reasons however, to explain the steady trickle of foreign investment in Laos and why more business people are being attracted to this little known and enigmatic country. For one thing the country, within certain parameters, really does offer one of the most liberal foreign investment policies in the region. It also offers peace, political stability, an appealing social climate, even the makings of a modest prosperity. Don't expect to turn a quick and easy profit though. As other business people have found out, the Lao are looking for long term investors, not bounty hunters or adventurers looking for 'El Dorado' in Asia.

The notion that the Lao might one day earn the right to handle their own business affairs or that they could be equal trading partners, never entered the colonial mind. The exploitation of the country's natural and human resources by empire builders and the requisitioning of the country by the superpowers has left its mark on the Lao who remain somewhat sceptical about the motives of foreigners, especially those who breeze in promising the world. A relatively untroubled few years of dealing at the business level with expats from various backgrounds has gone a long way towards ameliorating the suspicions of the Lao but they still remain cautious in their assessment of the sincerity of foreigners who come to Laos to do business. You certainly won't accomplish much if you arrive with a 'time is money' attitude, or a superior, 'let's go in there and show these people how it's done' approach to business.

Foreign companies or individuals are permitted to operate either joint ventures, with one or more domestic Lao investors, or fully owned new or branch or representative offices of foreign companies. Foreign investors are allowed to lease, though not exclusively own, land and to transfer their leasehold interest. Foreign investors are expected to give priority to Lao citizens when recruiting and hiring their employees but allowances are made for practical realities and companies have the perfect right to employ any skilled or specialist foreign personnel necessary.

The Lao preference for harmony and working things out by consensus is clearly spelt out in Article 21 of the country's Foreign Investment Code, which stipulates that in the event of disagreement between foreign investors and a Lao party, "The disputants should first seek to settle their differences through consultation or mediation."

177

The message to foreigners is clear: you are welcome to set up shop here, but don't rock the boat!

Trying to do business in any emerging Asian country can be a frustrating and time consuming affair for the uninitiated. Do as much research as you can before you arrive and, if necessary, set aside the full month of your business visa for a reconnaissance of the market potential of your enterprise. Take the opportunity to meet as many people as you can by getting to know different walks within the foreign community, not just those involved in business. Socialise at the expatriate clubs and generally make it known that you are a good listener, eager to learn from the experiences of other expats. People on the whole are very generous with their advice and living abroad often has the effect of making even the most standoffish person quite gregarious. Although the club's resident raconteur is likely to turn an account of a minor set back into a traumatic ordeal, if you make enough contacts within a broad spectrum of resident foreigners you will soon start forming a picture of what you can realistically expect from the country.

THE PECKING ORDER

No kind of business, however modest, can get off the ground without some form of official approval and an exacting and fairly lengthy period of screening in which you will have to meet with government representatives, present your project and credentials, be on your very best behaviour, and then wait patiently for a verdict.

Even in a country with strong socialist pretensions you will find that there is quite a traditional, almost Confucianist hierarchy of seniority, largely determined by age and length of service in the Party. If you are familiar with the language you will know right away who is being accorded the most respect from the forms of address being used. Otherwise, you will have to astutely observe the proceedings to determine who is deferred to most at the introduction stage, which officials are served coffee first and the titles – probably in both Lao and English – on the business cards which will be exchanged at the beginning. In most cases it won't take you long to see who the senior and subordinate people are.

It would be a gaffe indeed if a young expatriate, however well qualified, were to be over familiar or assertive with an older – and therefore senior in all respects – Lao official. The younger person would not only forfeit the respect of those present but would lose considerable ground in pressing his or her case.

It is wise, especially in the early stages, to cultivate good relations at all levels not just in the upper and middle echelons. An offended minion can just as easily sabotage, or cause lengthy and costly delays to a project as a more senior person.

NEGOTIATING TABLES

Personal contacts and the idea of getting to know those you deal with more intimately than is the usual practice in the West, are extremely important in Laos. The combative approach to business, which requires gaining an advantage over your negotiating partner or 'opponent,' of somehow coming out ahead, runs contrary to the Lao ethic in which parity is constantly emphasised. The idea of somebody losing out to a smarter, more aggressive and savvy operator is distasteful to the average Lao. In order that both parties feel that they have secured equal advantages for themselves, it is necessary and desirable when negotiating agreements and contracts to achieve consensus, which in turn implies harmonious relations.

You'll rarely get down to business immediately. What may seem like a lengthy preamble is the norm. These formalities are a good deal shorter than they used to be in the more courtly, not so distant past when guests could expect to be supplied with silver spittoons and trays of betel nut to munch on, and then served sherbet and tea. Communism's more pragmatic machinery did away with most of the formal preliminaries, although a residual etiquette involving coffee, inquiries into one's health and other civilities remain. Once this stage has been passed, someone will signal the start of the meeting proper and the agenda will be launched.

When presenting your material, try not to oversell yourself or make promises that you cannot fulfil. Outline realistic targets and attainable profits. The Lao will not be impressed by someone telling them that they can all be rich overnight. Assess your prospects for profit modestly, and while gently pushing the credentials of your company, never appear to be boasting. The hard sales pitch that worked wonders back home may be met with a stony silence here. The louder and more assertive you are, the less impact you will make.

Despite years of isolation and inexperience in dealing with foreigners on an equal footing, the Lao are not naive. Those who promise them the world will be dismissed as dreamers.

TRANSFER OF KNOW HOW

Foreign investment creates wealth which, at least in theory, percolates down to many levels and brings a certain internationalism with it, but it also provides access through the presence of skilled foreigners to technical knowledge, business expertise and opportunities for language acquisition. Foreigners are sometimes surprised, even put out, to find that they are expected to take on the mantle of teachers during their time in the country.

The Lao expectation is that you will be unstinting in the transfer of technological and management know-how, and working with a foreign company is often viewed as a learning situation, one that the government wholly endorses. This can place a heavy burden on the expat who may come to feel that he is spending an inordinately long time on the job training rather than creation of wealth side of things. Seen from a more positive perspective however, this is a company or individual's golden opportunity not only to improve the quality of staff but to be seen giving something back to the host country. To be investing in people, not just profit.

A government billboard gives a glimpse of the future in which trained Lao technicians run their own show without the help of foreigners.

REASONS FOR FAILURE

While most foreigners who arrive in Laos with a willingness to listen, learn and interact will stand a good chance of succeeding, there are others who leave in an angry and embittered frame of mind having achieved nothing. Some, though by no means all, of the common reasons for failure are listed below.

- Impatience and an inability to grasp the fact that there is often a hidden agenda, lurking like a subplot, beneath the surface of the negotiations.

- Trying to push things towards a speedy conclusion, to work within a strict time frame of all or nothing deadlines.

- A resentment at being expected to share knowledge and technical expertise. An 'If we tell them everything, we'll lose the edge' attitude.

- Not enough preparation in the early stages.

181

- An inability to assess the expectations and assumptions of the Lao.
- A propensity to delegate through an inflexible chain of command that excludes group consultation and decision making.
- A tendency to be 'high and mighty' when a decision or policy is politely questioned or challenged.
- A reluctance to socialise or have anything to do with staff during or after office hours.
- Slipping into a colonial mentality.

Those who involve themselves in the well being of their staff, allot time for staff training and welfare, socialise when the occasion arises and generally treat the staff as valued members of a team will soon find that they are at the helm of a loyal and hard working organisation, and that the odds of success begin to look exponentially more rosy.

A FRIEND IN NEED

To help you avoid some of the forgoing pitfalls, the services of a good secretary cannot be overestimated. A wisely chosen secretary or assistant will not only save you a good deal of time, money and effort, but possibly face as well. Apart from their normal duties, they may be able to advise on the right business tactics, recommend contacts if they already have some experience in working in your line of business, initiate you into the social niceties of dealing with different kinds of clients, gauge the prevailing mood surrounding a deal, act as translator for your paperwork and interpreter at meetings when the occasion arises. As a storehouse of accumulated knowledge and skilled in the finer points of public relations work, assistants of this calibre are more than worth their weight in gold.

CORRUPTING INFLUENCES

Gifts of one sort or the other are much appreciated by the Lao, and provided that they are given openly as rewards for work well done or as a natural mark of gratitude rather than as inducements, no one is likely to construe them as bribes.

The question of corruption, bribery, favouritism, funds for favours and 'present' giving is a delicate one. Corruption thrives, even in the most ethical of societies, when there are whopping great inequalities in income. In this respect, Lao is ripe for the practice. Salary levels for middle bureaucrats to ministers, for example, are a mere US$30–60 a month, a lot less than the monthly pickings of the average trishaw driver. Life can be very hard for people like civil servants, military personnel, teachers and underpaid doctors, who have to support families. As a result, many officials have other jobs in the private sector or in tourism. Residents recall a junior minister who until quite recently, could be seen selling quails' eggs at the Morning Market in Vientiane before turning up at his department to assume his official duties!

Despite occasional anti-corruption campaigning, the number of new houses and expensive import cars that have appeared from nowhere, tell their own story. It may be increasingly difficult as the private business sector grows for some officials to resist the temptation to charge kickbacks from local and foreign business people seeking documentation and permits.

Corruption in Laos is certainly no worse than anywhere else in Southeast Asia and, if the opinions of residents and visitors who do regular business here is anything to go by, it is if anything, a good deal 'cleaner' in this respect at present than most.

LAO STAFF

As dismissal of an under-performing member of staff is considered undesirable, it is important to hire the right staff. If someone is not pulling their weight, it is best to suggest that they transfer to a different section of the office. This has the merit of saving the person face but at the same time making it implicitly clear that the person is also to some extent on probation.

Lao who work for foreign companies soon learn the importance of punctuality. Providing that you are paying your staff a reasonable salary – foreign companies uniformly pay above par incomes – it is reasonable to insist that your staff only hold down one job so that they won't be rushing off before closing hours to fulfil commitments elsewhere. Put your cards very clearly on the table with anyone your are considering hiring to ensure that there will be no misunderstandings later on.

At government level there are few women in positions of authority. The private sector is different. There are a growing number of university and college educated young women, some of them skilled in one or more foreign languages, now joining the staffs of foreign and local firms. Shy, decorous and deferential by custom, many of these women are learning to balance the traditional characteristics of the Lao female with the realities of the workplace and their new job descriptions.

PERKS AND INCENTIVES

Good staff deserve to be rewarded from time to time as a sign of your appreciation, an indicator that all is going as it should be and as a motivator. While salary increases, bonuses, holiday and special leave perks are welcomed, more personal ways of promoting loyalty can also be shown.

Company events like the anniversary of its founding or the clinching of a new deal can be celebrated with a party in which staff can invite husbands and wives or other members of their families. Similar events can be held in the office or in a restaurant to celebrate things like birthdays and impending nuptials. Some companies are known to organise staff excursions or picnics to a not too distant religious sight or beauty spot. The ultimate, much coveted reward for service of course, is to send staff abroad to attend an all expenses paid training course.

DRESSING FOR WORK IN THE TROPICS

Appearances are important up to a point but dress codes are not as rigid as they often are elsewhere. Cleanliness is the main priority. Well pressed and ironed shirts, blouses, trousers and skirts – usually of the knee-length variety – in conservative colours and designs, are the norm.

Unless you are attending a crucial meeting, entertaining VIPs or official delegations, ties are not obligatory. Most bosses or senior management personnel have a jacket and tie on hand somewhere in the office as part of their dress ensemble but rarely get around to wearing them on a normal day unless the air-conditioning is arctic. A lot of Lao office and small factory staff will be working in humid conditions without the benefit of air-conditioning.

You don't often see people like waiters or shop assistants wearing a company uniform, although a number of Vientiane's medium sized international standard hotels provide their staff with them. People who dress too casually or in an overtly trendy manner may convey disrespect or frivolity and not be taken seriously.

TO BE AVOIDED

Inter-staff relations are just as important as public ones. There are a few basic ground rules applicable to much of Southeast Asia and Laos in particular, that have proved useful to foreigners and which are worth bearing in mind when dealing with the Lao at both the business and personal level.

- Never display anger, impatience or frustration. This is quite a tall order for foreigners used to clearing the air by letting off a bit of occasional steam.

- Avoid situations where people are likely to lose face, especially in front of others. It is not uncommon for people subjected to this form of humiliation to simply not turn up for work the next day.

- Good etiquette and courtesy are vital, especially when addressing older or more senior people who should always be deferred to.

- Never use the direct threat of dismissal as an inducement to get someone to work harder.

- Do not show preferential treatment to your foreign staff at the expense of their Lao co-workers.

- Avoid the colonial mentality. Any hint that you are playing the great white saviour role and that the locals are lucky to have landed a job with you will instantly alienate your entire staff and raise doubts about your business motives.

- Work at a steady, consistent pace. Don't rush your staff unless it is urgent.

LAOTIAN TIME

The much heard expression *Koi koi bai* – slowly, slowly – is associated not so much with taking things easy, but allowing enough time so that things can proceed at a natural speed and be done properly. The Lao are no more profligate with their time than anyone else but they have acquired a reputation for being extremely laid back,

even lackadaisical in their manner. What may have enormous appeal to tourists looking for relaxation in a rustic setting, can be frustrating to foreigners driven by deadlines, personal agendas and pressing appointments.

You may indeed find yourself subject to delays, the reasons for which will not always be obvious or even explained to you. At other times quick decisions may be deliberately avoided on the grounds that it would be imprudent not to allow more time for reflection. You will find that delays are tolerated to a much greater extent than you may be used to, and that the deferment or rescheduling of your carefully nurtured project is accepted by the Lao with a degree of equanimity which is often wrongly interpreted as apathy or *sangfroid*. The quality and conviviality of personal relations seems to be what counts most in Laos. If you are in a big hurry you would be better off opening your branch office or salesroom in Bangkok or Kuala Lumpur where people understand the concept of 'time is money' better.

Patience, respect and perseverance, as in all interpersonal matters in Laos, are the watchwords you should learn. Good business relations take time to mature so be prepared to commit plenty of it.

CULTURE TIPS

Anger: Should always be suppressed until you can find a way of releasing it safely on the tennis court or jogging circuit. Noisy, bad tempered foreigners will lose respect and discredit those associated with them.

Bonzes: The term used to describe a monk, often a novice one. You will see them in every major town or city in Laos. Lines of saffron-robed bonzes filing along the streets at dawn has now become almost a cliche of travel in the East.

Bargaining: More than just a question of getting a good deal, bargaining has become a social custom which you are expected, even encouraged, to do. It has some of the same pleasure that public auctions carry.

Criticising: Should be done with the utmost discretion and tact, and never in front of other people. If you need to criticise someone, take them aside and politely and obliquely draw their attention to the matter.

Discos: Look out for special 'dance nights' and cabarets in hotels and large restaurants. When attending discos, forget everything this book has told you about the Lao people: discos are loud, brash, boozy and asphyxiating. They are also great fun with DJs and live bands pumping out nonstop sounds.

Eating: One of the pleasures of any Southeast Asian country. Knives and forks are not commonly used, except in foreign style restaurants. A large spoon is the norm. Chopsticks are used for some dishes. Sticky rice is eaten with the fingers.

Friends: Despite their natural reserve and moderation in all things, the Lao are a warm, convivial and spirited people. You will have few problems making friends in Laos.

Gifts: The custom of gift giving exists in Laos but it is nowhere near as complicated as it is in some Asian countries like Japan or Korea. The fine line between gift giving and bribery in business circles is a question of value and timing.

Home Visits: Visiting someone's home provides one of the best insights into a culture you could hope for. Shoes should be removed before entering the house. A small gift would certainly be appreciated but it is not the normal custom. Try to join in the spirit of the occasion by sampling every dish or drink that is offered, unless there is some religious prohibition that prevents you.

Indigenous Cultures: Laos has some of the most varied and authentic ethnic minorities in the whole of Southeast Asia. With the changes affecting the region their cultures are as fragile as the existence of any endangered species of wildlife. Try to respect these fascinating micro-cultures as part of our world heritage before they vanish forever.

Karst: The name given to a landscape shaped by limestone deposits. Terrain of this sort is characterised by steep, conical hills, sharp ridges, underground rivers and sink holes. Laos can boast many of these beautiful formations which are so reminiscent of Chinese ink wash paintings.

Khene: The national instrument of Laos looks slightly Andean in appearance with its sets of bamboo and reed pipes of various lengths which are strapped together and then blown into by the player.

Lao Ramayana: The Lao version of the Indian epic the *Ramayana*, or *Ramakien*, can sometimes be seen at festival times or on other special occasions. The original, written by the poet Valmiki some 2000 years ago, runs to 48,000 lines. Performances these days tend to be abridged but well worth seeing for their gorgeous costumes, mythical settings and stylised gestures. The epic has often been compared to the works of Homer.

Laterite: Laterisation is a process of soil erosion caused by warm, moist conditions which deprive tropical soil of its nutrients. You will see a lot of this red earth in Laos. Many ancient temples were built of stone made from laterite.

Munitions: There are still many unexploded munitions lying around to make rambles a risky pastime in many areas. You should never wander off into forests, uncultivated fields or thickets on your own or at whim. The highest concentration of bombs and other forms of live explosives are found in Xieng Khouane, the provinces of Saravan and Champassak and along the Lao stretch of the Ho Chi Minh Trail.

Pirogues: A type of canoe found throughout Indo-China. Sometimes called dugouts, they are often still made in the traditional way by hollowing out a tree trunk.

Prostitution: It does exist in Laos but you would hardly know. Whereas in Thailand the world's oldest profession is perfectly legal, in Laos the opposite applies. Women caught engaging in prostitution are liable to jail sentences of between six months and three years. Apart from the fact that Laos is and always has been a deeply traditional society, the Lao government is determined to avoid an AIDS epidemic on the scale of its more liberal neighbour.

Rice: You don't have to like rice to survive in Laos but it certainly helps. Sticky or glutinous rice *(khao nyao)* is the one the Lao are most partial to. Rice flour *(Khao beua)* as well as toasted, mashed and grilled rice are also popular. Rice cakes are sold in the markets. Other forms of pasta are *khao poon Chin*, a transparent Chinese vermicelli known in the West as 'cellophane noodles' and its Lao equivalent *Khao poon*.

Rainy Season: Be well prepared for it. Waterproof shoes, a folding raincoat and a good umbrella are the minimum requirements. The humidity and low cloud bring out swarms of mosquitoes, especially at night so have coils, mosquito nets and electric fans at hand.

Saunas: In a country where you are not supposed to show your anger, vent your frustrations publicly or speak your mind without grave lose of face, Vientiane's herbal saunas are great unwinders, a chance to sweat out the week's accumulated anxieties and reflect on a better modus operandi for the next one.

Snooker: Aficionados will be delighted to find indoor and outdoor snooker tables all over the place. Quite how the game was introduced to the country remains a mystery.

Textiles: One of the best buys in Laos. Light, portable and affordable they make perfect presents for friends back home who won't believe that you only paid US$20 for that exquisite silk wall hanging. The colours, designs and applications are endless. Artificial dyes are mostly used these days as they save time. Natural dyes need to be soaked many times before they become colourfast. Watch out for cotton substitutes and synthetic yarns though. All very nice looking but not the same.

U.S. Relations: Despite the suffering and plight caused by U.S. military policy during the Vietnam War, the Lao hold almost no grudge against America in general and Americans in particular.

This often surprises and touches visitors from the States who expect at some time during their stay to be held personally to account for the past. Interestingly enough, the American Embassy in Vientiane was allowed to remain open even during the early days of the revolutionary government, a situation that has continued to this day.

Victory Gate: Also known as the Patuxai, Anousavari and in some French guide books, the Monument aux Morts, this imposing memorial to those Lao who died in the various wars of liberation is, rather ironically, strongly reminiscent of the Arc de Triomphe in Paris, though this one is finished off in concrete. And therein lies a story. Begun in the early 1960s, the money-strapped Lao authorities, eager to have the monument finished as quickly as possible, requisitioned several tonnes of U.S. cement, supposedly part of an aid package earmarked for the building of a new airport. (Now you know why the locals affectionately refer to the monument as 'the vertical runway'!)

Water: Should never be drunk straight from the tap. Politely decline a glass too if it is offered in someone's house or at a roadside restaurant or stall, even if it means causing offence. Make sure if you order mineral water in a restaurant or cafe that the cap is still securely sealed when it is brought to you. Guests are usually offered bottled drinks at home. If you are not sure what to order outside, ask for *nam saa*, hot tea. Iced coffee *(ooliiang)* is very popular but is usually prepared with unsterilised cubes.

Xenophobia: The Lao are not overtly xenophobic but centuries of incursions, reprisals, and exploitation at the hands of foreigners have left their mark on these temperamentally prudent and wary people.

A seated Buddha made from bronze at Wat Phra Keo in Vientiane.

CULTURAL QUIZ

Although incidents and the order in which they happened have been changed, all the situations here actually happened. In fact some of them, with minor variations, are recurring situations in the eventful and challenging lives that most expatriates live here. Once you have put in a bit of time in the country and learnt some Lao ways you will be better equipped to handle the unpredictable without being too flustered. In the meantime, try to imagine how you would cope or extrapolate yourself from the circumstances below with your pride and face more or less intact.

There are no definitive solutions to working yourself out of the following situations but a combination of common sense and astute cultural evaluation will give you a head start. You might think that nothing like this could possibly happen to you, but just wait and see!

SITUATION ONE

A friend tells you that he recently bought a small Buddha image in Luang Prabang in a private sale. He put the statue in his bag which he placed in the basket of his bicycle. As he was peddling along the street he felt an irresistible force pulling his handlebars to the right. Unable to control his bike he was obliged to stop and push it back to the hotel. When he explained the incident to the manager of the hotel where he was staying and showed him the image, he was told that it must have been stolen from the Tham Ting Cave and was refusing to be taken away. Your friend asks you for advice. What do you tell him?

A Laugh the incident off and tell him to be more rational.

B Contact the authorities and let them make a decision.

C Try to find the person he bought it from and explain the situation.

D Tell him to replace the object himself with a suitable offering.

Comments

Religious objects do occasionally get stolen from temples and sacred sites. Whether they protest the abduction themselves is another question. Option A is definitely not cool, at least in the company of Lao. Never scoff at the possibility of strange, unaccountable phenomena. Option C will probably fall on deaf ears.

Choice B is by far the best one. The Ministry of Information and Culture will listen to the story seriously and be grateful to have the image returned safely. Option D could draw unwanted attention to your friend if he were to be seen skulking around with something like this in his bag. He might even be accused of stealing the object himself.

SITUATION TWO

You discover a large snake in the grounds of your house. Quickly summoning your gardener you ask him to kill the reptile as quickly as he can. Instead of carrying out your request, he appears to be looking for an alternative home for the said serpent: in the field at the end of your plot or over the fence in the garden of your next door neighbour. If your gardener proposed to eat the thing or remove its spleen and sell it to the local practitioner of Chinese medicine, you could understand. But what precisely is going on, and what should you do next?

- **A** Insist on the execution and stand by while it is carried out.
- **B** Kill the creature yourself.
- **C** Release it onto somebody else's land and trust that it doesn't come back.
- **D** Let the gardener handle the situation himself and hope for the best.

Comments

You shouldn't push the gardener to do something that he plainly feels uncomfortable about. In fact he is simply following the Buddhist precept of not killing another living creature which most Lao will stick to if it is deemed pointless to do so. Option B might be a bit drastic and cast you in a rather ruthless light. Option C is a possibility but is it fair to possibly expose someone else to the same shock? In this case it really does seem that your only choice is the fourth one. Trust the gardener's judgement but keep your eyes open.

SITUATION THREE

You stop a samlor driver, tell him clearly where you wish to go, agree on the fare and set off. When you arrive at your destination the man demands an extra 1000 kip on the grounds that he didn't know how far it was. Didn't you go through all this beforehand with him? Is it a genuine underestimate or does he do this with every gullible foreigner he picks up?

    A Vent your anger by telling him you were not born yesterday and, in any case, both parties agreed on the fare at the onset, so what's he talking about?

    B Its too hot to stand around wrangling over a few kip. Pay him what he asks and have done with it.

    C Stick to the original deal and only pay the agreed fare.

    D Compromise and pay him half of what he demands.

Comments

If the driver seems genuinely confused and the distance turns out to be longer than both of you imagined, options B or D would be the fairest. If you think you are being had, opt for C. The first option is rather futile.

SITUATION FOUR

You are going to Bangkok for a long weekend. You have been working especially hard recently and you and your wife, who has suffered from your irascible moods at home, are both looking forward to the break and the opportunity to do nothing for a few days. On the day before you leave, a Lao colleague asks you if you wouldn't mind picking up a few things for him while you are in Thailand. Shopping for other people is the last thing you want to do on your precious, long awaited weekend. What can you do to get out of it?

    A Flatly refuse.

    B Apologise and make an excuse to the effect that you don't think you will be in a position to help.

C Turn the whole thing into an impossible joke and say that your wife would fly into a fit if you deviated from your original leisure plans.

D Agree to the request.

Comments

Option A is what you would most like to do but would seem brusque and impolite. And besides, you have to collaborate with this person professionally. Choice B is the most viable if you are determined to preserve your plans. Choice C may not be understood or, more to the point, believed. D is the altruists option, but beware that you might be setting a precedent here.

SITUATION FIVE

While you are discussing business with an important client in your office you ask your assistant to bring in some documents. She seems to have been gone for an inordinately long time, but when she does appear the papers are the wrong ones. You issue the same request with, alas, the same result. Is this a case for impatience or restraint? Are you going to publicly berate the women, try again to secure the precious papers or do it yourself?

A Write down the details of the document you are looking for on a piece of paper and cross your fingers.

B Stomp off in a huff and find the damn things yourself.

C Politely excuse yourself and go and help your assistant hunt for them.

D Reprimand her inefficiency.

Comments

Certainly not options B and D which would lead to instant loss of face. Laos is a small place, news travels fast, gossip even faster and reputations have to be protected. Also, if your client is Lao such gross tactlessness could easily backfire on you.

Option A is a possibility, but what happens if she still can't find the documents you need? Choice C may be the best as it will save time and show what a jolly decent and cooperative sort of boss you are. You can tackle the assistant later when you are alone if you feel there is cause for grievance or if this is a recurring situation with her, in which case you may be forced to seriously review the question of her future with the company.

SITUATION SIX

You are ordering dinner at a street stall in the Morning Market with a group of friends, none of whom including yourself, can read the handwritten menu that is placed in front of you. Deciding that its either a case of lucky dip or don't eat, you point hopefully to four items and nod affirmatively for the order. What turns up is clearly meat, but not one, after a few moments of experimental prodding, sniffing and

consultation, that anyone can recognise. You begin to recall now that rats, decomposed swallows and even pangolins are standard fare in Laos. Suddenly none of you feel quite as hungry as you did before. A decision has to be made before the food gets cold.

A Have the dishes removed and move on to a safer bet like a French restaurant or pizzeria.

B Put a brave face on your reservations and plunge into the dishes with gusto.

C Call the waitress or cook over and go through a pantomime of every edible animal and bird you can think of to establish the identity of the dish.

D Order some extra dishes to camouflage the ones you will be leaving untouched.

Comments

Option A would be insulting but also wasteful. Choice B is perfectly viable as the dishes in all probability will turn out to be perfectly alright and the chances of eating rodents, exotic dishes or endangered species at a busy city eatery are less likely than in a provincial town or village. Option C, if you are good at this sort of thing, would offend no one and provide some free amusement for other customers. Somebody might even come forward to offer an explanation. Choice D is a good compromise that will not upset the stall keeper or your fragile stomachs.

SITUATION SEVEN

Your car has come off the road in a remote country area and lodged itself in a ditch. A group of locals eventually appear and help you heave-ho the vehicle back onto the road. How do you show your appreciation?

A Thrust a handful of banknotes into the pocket of the villager who showed the most initiative and ask him to divide the money up later.

B Shake each of their hands, thank them profusely and then leave.

C Take someone's name and address with a view to sending some kind of gift later on.

D Fish around for useful items to pass on to them such as food, supplies or other tokens of appreciation.

Comments

Depending on the number of people, your assessment of their characters and background, any of the four options are variously acceptable. Money though, is always less personal and may even be refused on principal.

SITUATION EIGHT

You took some photographs of young novice monks while you were on a trip. You promised to send them copies and have dutifully dispatched them. Two or three weeks later you receive a letter from one of the monks saying that his family is very poor and that it is too expensive for them to support him at a university. Could you send him money and, if possible, a Japanese made radio? Are you being taken for a ride or is this a genuine plea for help? And what about the radio?

A Write back and tell him that you are not a registered charity.

B Send either the money, the radio or both.

C Try to explain that it is far nicer to send photos than money. Would he like some extra prints?

D Ignore the letter altogether.

Comments

Option A may satisfy you if you feel offended or disappointed by the approach, but will probably not be understood by the young man in question. The second choice is a possibility but be prepared to receive more requests in the future. Option C is the most reasonable and diplomatic response. The last choice may also be a possibility if you feel that you have done quite enough already and that the person is genuinely taking advantage of you.

SITUATION NINE

You are taken aside and told in the manner of an old and esteemed friend that a certain person has passed away. In fact, you only knew him slightly, and then only for a very short time. You are eager to show the correct degree of sympathy and do not wish to belittle the person's death and the family's own grief but, to be quite frank, you would prefer not to attend the funeral of a barely known acquaintance. What would be the correct line of action to take?

A   Offer polite condolences and then change the subject.

B   Have someone take over some flowers and a card to the family.

C   Declaim any serious relationship with the deceased.

D   Attend the funeral.

Comments

D would be the noblest choice. Apart from reflecting well on you, the larger the attendance at a funeral, the more prestige the family will accrue on behalf of the deceased. Option B would also be acceptable showing that you have responded with more than just words. Choices A and C would project you as callous and ill bred.

SITUATION TEN

Your driver and guide on a journey upcountry keeps making unscheduled stopovers in villages and roadside stalls to buy, pick up and deliver quantities of rice, durians and sundry edibles. What exactly is going on? And what, if anything, should you do?

A Tell them this is not a shopping expedition at your expense and to stick to the original schedule.

B Say nothing.

C Ask them if this is normal procedure and what it all means.

D Treat it all as part of the upcountry experience and join in with a little unofficial shopping of your own.

Comments

Option A would not only be rude but counter productive in the long run. B would be perfectly acceptable but won't satisfy your curiosity. The best choices would be either C or D, whichever suits you best. Option D, providing that you are not in a rush, will let you enjoy the diversion and enter into the spirit of things. Guides and drivers in the remoter parts of the provinces often take the opportunity to stock up on supplies which may not be available back in town or in their village. Fruit and vegetables may also be a lot cheaper and fresher in these areas.

FURTHER READING

Bock, Carl, *Temples and Elephants*. Oxford. A grumpy, 19th century traveller's experiences in Siam and Laos.

Cheesman, Patricia, *Lao Textiles: Ancient Symbols, Living Art*. White Lotus, Bangkok, 1988. Good introduction to Lao weaving arts by leading expert on the subject.

Cummings, Joe, *Lonely Planet Laos*. Lonely Planet Publications, 1996. The best known travel guide to Laos.

Dommen, Arthur J, *Laos: Keystone of Indochina*. Westview, Boulder, Colorado, 1985. An authoritative analysis of the country's political and strategic importance to the region.

Evans, Grant & Rowley, Kevin, *Red Brotherhood at War – Vietnam, Cambodia and Laos since 1975*. Versa, 1990. Meticulous analysis of the aftermath of revolution.

Groslier, Bernard Philipe, *The Art of Indochina*. London, 1962. A classic on the subject.

Hall, D. G. E., *A History of Southeast Asia*. St. Martins Press, New York, 1981. A good, general introduction to the region.

Hamilton, Wanda, *Favourite Stories from Laos*. Heinemann Asia, Singapore, 1990. Two slim, illustrated volumes in series for children.

Hoshino, Tatsuo, Marcus, Russell, *Lao for Beginners*. Charles E. Tuttle, Tokyo, 1993.

Hoskins, John & Hopkins, Allen W, *The Mekong: A River and Its People*. Post Publishing Co., Bangkok, 1991.

Lewis, Norman, *A Dragon Apparent: Travels in Cambodia, Laos and Vietnam*. Eland, London, 1982. A classic of literary travel. Eminent writer Lewis's account of his journey through the region in the early 1950s.

LNCCI, *Lao National Chamber of Commerce And Industry Directory*. Vientiane. A useful reference for business-people.

Mansfield, Stephen, Hall, Tim, *Laos A Portrait*. Elseworth Books Ltd., Hong Kong, 1995. A large format photo book with text.

Mansfield, Stephen, *Cultures of the World – Laos*. Times Editions, Singapore, 1997. An illustrated, reference book on Laos written for young teens and educators.

Ngaosyvathn, Mayoury, *Lao Women Yesterday And Today*. State Publishing Enterprise, Vientiane, 1995. Insights into the life and minds of the Lao women.

Robbins, Christopher, *The Ravens*. Entertaining and revealing look at the CIA's secret war in Laos and the controversial role played by the pilots that flew the Air America rigs.

Sing, Phia, *Traditional Recipes of Laos*. Prospect Books, England, 1995. An engaging collection of recipes by the late Master of Ceremonies and Chef at the Royal Palace in Luang Prabang.

Stewart, Lucretia, *Tiger Balm: Travels in Laos, Vietnam and Cambodia*. Chatto & Windus, 1992. Contemporary travels in Indochina from a woman's point of view.

Sluiter, Liesbeth, *The Mekong Currency*. Per/Terra, Bangkok, 1992. An original study of the river and its people.

Soukbandith, Bounmy, *Modern English-Lao, Lao-English Dictionary*. PO Box 40021, San Diego, CA 92164, USA. Excellent, up to date work.

Stuart-Fox, Martin, *Laos: Politics, Economics and Society*. Frances Pinter, London, 1986. Authoritative work by eminent Australian Lao specialist and academic.

Werner, Klaus, *Learning Lao For Everybody*. State Printing Enterprise, 1994. A pocket sized introduction to the language.

Women's International Group, *Vientiane Guide*. Updated each year and compiled by a non-profit organisation, contains useful information, addresses and announcements for both residents and travellers.

Zickgraf, Ralph, *Places And Peoples of the World, Laos*. Chelsea House, New York, 1991. An easy reader introduction.

THE AUTHOR

Stephen Mansfield was born in England but has spent over ten years living in Asia. Other homes abroad have included Cairo and Barcelona. He worked for many years as an EFL teacher and in educational administration, an experience that gave him the opportunity to meet and interact with people from numerous cultural backgrounds before turning to full time photo journalism.

As a freelance writer and photographer, his work has appeared in over 80 newspapers and magazines worldwide. He has written at length on subjects ranging from travel, politics, food, and the problems facing ethnic minorities around the world, to ecology. A keen interest in world affairs and culture has led him at one time or another into encounters with figures as diverse as Salvador Dali and Aung San Suu Kyi. He is the author of several books including a guidebook to Myanmar, *Birmanie: Le Temps Suspendu*, with Michel Huteau, and *Tokyo On The Loop: A Photographic Journey Around The Yamanote Line*. He is generally regarded as one of the foremost travel and culture writers on Laos. He is the author and photo contributor to *Laos A Portrait*. Apart from being the author and photographer for *Culture Shock! Laos*, he has written and illustrated *Cultures of the World: Laos*, also published by Times Editions.

He now divides his time between a new home in South West France, helping out looking after two tri-lingual children, and his writing and photography projects in Southeast Asia and other parts of the world.

INDEX